THE
LITTLE
BOOK
OF
IRISH
BOXING

BARRY FLYNN

The
History
Press
Ireland

To Katrina, Méabh and Deirbhile

First published 2015

The History Press Ireland
50 City Quay
Dublin 2
Ireland
www.thehistorypress.ie

British Library Cataloguing in Publication Data.
A catalogue record for this book is available from the British Library.

ISBN 978 1 84588 876 3

Typesetting and origination by The History Press

Printed and bound in Great Britain by TJ International Ltd, Padstow

CONTENTS

1. The Eighteenth and Nineteenth Centuries   4

2. The 1900 and 1910s   13

3. The 1920s and 1930s   16

4. The 1940s   29

5. The 1950s   37

6. The 1960s   57

7. The 1970s   72

8. The 1980s   90

9. The 1990s   109

10. The Twenty-First Century   125

1

THE EIGHTEENTH AND NINETEENTH CENTURIES

PETER CORCORAN – HEAVYWEIGHT CHAMPION OF ENGLAND

Born in Athy, County Kildare, in 1749, Peter Corcoran held the distinction of becoming the first Irishman to claim the heavyweight title of England. Rumoured to have fled Ireland after killing a man in a dispute over a woman, Corcoran found work as a coal-heaver in London where his feats of strength enthralled great crowds. When he came to the attention of Captain Dennis O'Kelly in the 1760s, Corcoran's career as a bare-knuckle fighter took off. O'Kelly was a dubious rogue and a gambler of note who oversaw the rise of Corcoran and his eventual challenge for the English title against Bill Darts at the Epsom Downs racecourse on 18 May 1771. That fight was for £200 and tens of thousands craned their necks to witness the battle. However, O'Reilly had paid Darts a small fortune to throw the fight, or to 'fight booty' as it was then known. Accordingly, within a minute, Darts, on shipping a punch to the nose, surrendered and Corcoran was declared the champion.

Corcoran was to defend that crown on five occasions and he purchased the Black Horse Inn in London's East End with the proceeds from his career. His title, however, was lost in suspicious circumstances to Henry Sellars in 1776 in the eighteenth round of their bloody battle. This time it was thought that Corcoran had 'fought booty' as part of a betting coup. Such was the 'upset' that Pierce Egan, in his 1820 book *Boxiana*, noted, 'The poor Paddies were literally ruined as many of them had backed their darling boy with every last farthing they possessed.' In defeat, Corcoran became yesterday's man and his fortune dwindled away to nothing. He died in poverty in London in 1781, aged 32.

THE SWEET SCIENCE IN THE EMERALD ISLE

Daniel Mendoza was considered the father of modern boxing and had a profound influence on the development of the sport as a science. Born in Spain in 1764, Mendoza published his book *The Art of Boxing* in 1789, which expounded the theory that speed, footwork and technique could prevail over sheer brute strength. Standing at merely 5ft 7in, Mendoza used his boxing theory to great effect and won the English middleweight title in 1789, when he defeated the then champion Richard Humphries. On becoming champion, Mendoza toured the British Isles, showing off his skills as part of Astery's Travelling Circus. On arriving in Dublin in 1791, Mendoza established a boxing school for budding pugilists in Dame Street. It was here that Mendoza was to be confronted by 'a swell of great weight and little prudence', named Squire Fitzgerald, the so-called 'Pride of Ireland'. With the backing of, amongst others, the Duke of Leinster, the Earl of Ormonde and Lord Westmeath, who put up a £50 purse for a fight between the two men, Fitzgerald insulted Mendoza's Jewish background and challenged him for his title. The two met in Dublin on 2 August and the fight lasted twenty rounds before Fitzgerald surrendered in exhausted disarray, apologising afterwards to his opponent for his offensive pre-fight insults.

THE LEGEND OF DAN DONNELLY

> Come all ye true-bred Irishmen, I hope you will draw near
> And likewise pay attention, to the lines that I have here.
> It is as true a story, as ever you did hear
> Of how Donnelly fought Cooper, at the Curragh of Kildare.

Ireland's most famous bare-knuckle fighter was the celebrated Dan Donnelly. Donnelly was born in Townsend Street in Dublin in 1788, the seventh of nine children. He began his prize-fighting career when, as a mere 15-year-old, he gained a reputation with his fists after humbling an English sailor who had insulted his father in a Dublin bar. His career flourished under joint-promoters Captain Kelly and Captain Barclay and he became renowned worldwide. On 13 December 1815, heavy rain fell on the Curragh, County Kildare, but that did not stop thousands making their way there to watch Donnelly fight the English champion George Cooper. Despite the long odds, Donnelly prevailed after eleven rounds with a final punch that broke his opponent's jaw.

When the victory was declared, it was greeted with the 'loudest and longest cheer ever heard on the Curragh of Kildare'. The natural amphitheatre where the fight took place was renamed 'Donnelly's Hollow' in honour of his victory.

Donnelly's career flourished in England where, in 1819, he defeated the highly rated Tom Oliver in the thirty-fourth round of their battle. Afterwards, Donnelly was knighted for his efforts by the then Prince Regent, the future George IV. Unfortunately, Donnelly's private life did not match his fighting skills. Through heavy drinking, he squandered ownership of four pubs and was to die in poverty of alcoholism. When he passed away in 1820, tens of thousands of mourners filled the streets of Dublin to attend his funeral. He was buried in Bully's Acre in Kilmainham but his body was stolen by grave robbers. When the corpse was eventually re-discovered, it was missing its right arm, which was found to be in the possession of a Dublin anatomist named Hall. The limb was then preserved with lead paint and exhibited around Britain and Ireland. In 1904, the arm was bought by Hugh McAlevey and put on display in his public house, the Duncairn Arms in Belfast. Later it was bought by Kildare boxing fan Jim Byrne and displayed in his restaurant, The Hideout, in Kilcullen, before becoming the chief attraction of 'The Fighting Irishmen' exhibition in New York in 2006.

A BRUTAL EXHIBITION IN COUNTY MEATH

The normally quiet hamlet of Greenogue, County Meath, had its peace disturbed on the morning of Tuesday 27 March 1860, when Paddy Murphy and Andrew Moore met for a £100 purse. The two 'celebrated Dublin bullies' attracted 3,000 spectators to a local field well away from the eyes and ears of the constabulary and betting was said to be brisk as the men appeared stripped to the waist. After some preliminary sparring, the fight began in earnest and lasted a full half hour before Moore, 'The Black Diamond', was declared the winner. In a final desperate attack, Murphy tripped and dislocated his shoulder and was led away sporting a badly disfigured jaw. The *Freeman's Journal* reported that, 'It is to be regretted that the police were not able to ascertain the time the place selected for this fight, so as to prevent the brutal display,' adding that such fights were 'fortunately extremely rare in this country'.

PUGILISM ON THE SABBATH DAY – *THE IRISH TIMES* 1864

'A printed handbill has been placed in our possession, announcing that a pugilistic encounter will take place on Sunday next, 9 October, at Foxrock. The combatants are named as JOHN WALSH, alias WAPS, and SAM BARTLETT, sail-maker, and the wager is fixed at twenty pounds. The challenge, it is stated, was given and accepted at a public house in George's Street, Kingstown, on Tuesday last. Hitherto, this country has not been disgraced by such brutalising exhibitions. It is evident, however, that some persons do intend to desecrate the Sabbath Day and to disgrace the pleasant and peaceful neighbourhood of Foxrock by a low imitation of an exhibition that is at best savage and brutal. We now call on the police authorities to prevent so great a scandal. If this "fight" is permitted to take place, the suburbs of Dublin will, on every Sabbath Day, be infested with crowds of dissipated and daring men, assembled to witness the most savage and degrading exhibition that can be conceived, and the worst characters of Dublin will sally forth, nominally to see a fight, but in reality to plunder.'

PRIZE FIGHTING AND DOG FIGHTING

A crowd of 600 spectators gathered at the Seventh Lock beside the Royal Canal in Dublin's north side on Sunday 28 November 1876 in anticipation of a fight between two local pugilists. At stake was the princely sum of £25 for the rematch of the two protagonists, who worked in the Cattle Market and who had fought two months previously. With the crowd assembled, news came through that one of the pugilists had had an attack of cold feet and had wisely forgone the rematch. Despite the cancellation, a fight involving two dogs was arranged to entertain the crowds. A ring was formed and two men came forward, one a butcher from Bray and the other a man from Thomas Street in Dublin, with their straining dogs. The dog fight lasted for forty-five minutes, by which time the butcher's dog lay mutilated and almost lifeless on the ground. His master, however, enraged by his dog's poor performance, dragged his animal by its throat to the water and held its head beneath the surface until it was dead. Despite the protests of some in the crowd, the butcher remained oblivious to pleas to save the poor dog. The crowd dispersed at pace as news of a police raid was circulated.

AMERICAN PRIZE FIGHT –
LIMERICK MAN DEFEATED

Two hundred 'gentlemen of leisure' witnessed the secret and illegal clash between Limerick's Jim Frawley and Charles Norton, the lightweight champion of New York, at a warehouse in Coney Island in May 1882. Known as the 'Veteran Irish Pugilist', Frawley lasted merely three rounds, much to the disappointment of the vociferous Irish supporters in attendance. Frawley, who had been accompanied into the ring by his seconds, Mike Noonan and Tim Hussey, sported gleaming white britches with green trimmings. However, Norton drew first blood in the contest with a right uppercut to Frawley's lip. As the first round concluded, Norton was very much in the ascendancy. By the third round, Frawley was a well-beaten man and his seconds wisely threw their sponge into the ring to signal that the fight was over. As the Limerick man sat on his stool gasping for air, the patrons scattered with great haste as mounted police raided the warehouse. Amid the commotion, Frawley was arrested and taken by carriage to Bergen Street police station in Brooklyn, where he was charged with partaking in an illegal pugilistic gathering. Insult was duly added to the injury that Frawley had suffered at the hands of Norton when a sentence of three months' imprisonment was handed down for his participation in the fight.

WOMEN'S PUGILISM IN VICTORIAN DUBLIN

On Saturday 4 August 1883, the *Irish Examiner* reported with great distaste an episode of what it labelled 'a disgraceful display of female pugilism', which had taken place in Capel Street the previous Tuesday. The article continued, 'A pair of fishwives hailing from Pill Lane fought for the space of half an hour in the aforementioned street'. However, if the unregulated display of fighting was not bad enough, the newspaper reserved special criticism for 'the large crowd of observers who, instead of mediating as peacemakers, spurred the protagonists on and suffered them to fight it out to the bitter end'. Notably, the article did not mention which of the protagonists had been declared victorious at the end of what must have been a gruelling contest.

PRIZE FIGHTING IN SKIBBEREEN

The Temperance Hall in Skibbereen, County Cork, was hired on Sunday 1 November 1885 for the purposes of a 'scientific lecture, illustrated with experiments'. What actually occurred was far from scientific. Between the hours of eleven and twelve o'clock in the morning, a local tinsmith and a butcher battled for a £20 prize in front of an intoxicated crowd. The noise created by the masses in attendance alerted local residents who ran to the police barracks to exclaim that a 'bloody murder was taking place'. Immediately, Sergeant McGrath, together with constables Fanning and Deacon, went to the hall only to find that the disturbance had concluded. On making enquiries, McGrath was told that the 'lecture' had been interrupted by some 'drunken roughs' and that the temperance men had had great difficulty in ejecting them from the hall. Despite the tall tale, it was reported that the tinsmith had won the battle and claimed the purse.

JOHN L. SULLIVAN AT THE ULSTER HALL – DECEMBER 1887

'The lovers of sport in Belfast truly got their hearts' delight last Saturday night 17th inst Mr. John L. Sullivan, the world-renowned champion of the gloves, appeared for the first time before a Belfast audience at the Ulster Hall, and seldom has such a scene been witnessed. Indeed, it might be said that from the moment the local manager, Mr. John Shorthouse, issued the announcement that Yankee Sullivan would visit Belfast and give a few tips to "the boys", the greatest interest was taken by the lovers of the "noble art" in all classes of society. When the tickets were sent out a regular stampede was made for them and everything that followed on Saturday was in keeping with the keen public demand. Long before the hour of commencement of the fun at the Ulster Hall, the venue was besieged, and when the doors were flung open the ticket issuers and collectors had their hands full. Nevertheless, the utmost order prevailed, and the slightest semblance of roughness – something naturally to be anticipated on such an occasion – was not apparent at any of the entrances.

'It is true, however, that quite a few of the audience did treat themselves to better seats than they were entitled to and some in their anxiety to see the champion stood on their seats, with the result being that some were indeed broken. No notice of the noisy affair, but for the occasional smile on the face of the pugilists who were facing each other, was evident amid the cracking and crashing sounds as the aforementioned seats succumbed to gravity. Things were somewhat different in Dublin when no less than 65 constables had to be called in to preserve order at the Gaiety Theatre during the exhibition by John L. and this speaks loudly of the past and future conduct of Belfast audiences. To facilitate the exhibition, a tidy roped-off platform had been erected a short distance from the orchestra for the performers and this attracted the gaze of all the assembled mass. This platform was all that could have been desired and at the outset it required only a little sawdust, and a little late on some more was added to make it thoroughly comfortable for those engaged upon it. Owing to the great crush outside the venue, it was almost eight o'clock before proceedings could be commenced. When the last of the numbers were put up in the hall, it was actually crammed to its capacity, and if we make exception for the shouting of the vendors of the programmes and photos of the "Bruiser" there was nothing to object to. Almost all hands enjoyed a whiff of the weed, as John L. has no objection to smoking. Indeed, it was a rare night when one considers that all classes of society were present and it was impossible to observe even an effort on the part of those with anti-boxing tendencies to make themselves heard, many of whom, no doubt, were in attendance building up the courage to view the punishment dished out by the protagonists.

'It is recorded that recently even men of the cloth had witnessed the struggle between classic fight between Messrs. Sayers and Heenan, and few could have doubted this when surveying the assemblage congregated to greet Mr. Sullivan and his troupe on Saturday. The first two into the arena were a Mr. Hopkins and Mr. Murphy, with Mr. Philips keeping the time. The usual formality of the shaking of the hands was gone through and both youngsters being laced up began to go at each other with great gusto. Their display was fair enough, with Hopkins having the advantage if anything. The fight lasted three rounds and then Jack Hickey and Jim Kendrick appeared for their bout, in which great interest was shown. Indeed, it was a rare treat to see Hickey at work and at the end of each round he was warmly applauded. His backhanders were clever and in point he was much superior to his adversary. And then the moment arrived as the Master of Ceremonies, Mr. Gallagher, introduced Sullivan who was warmly received with all rising to their feet and cheering enthusiastically. The champion responded and thanked the crowd for their warm reception. He had left Boston on 27th October and had come to this country to see the class of men we had here. He said that he hoped to have the pleasure of meeting the victor of the coming fight between Kilraine and Smith – and indeed Mitchell – with whom he would be meeting in the near future. Well, all these men will soon have the chance to test themselves against Sullivan, with the result a sure and foregone conclusion in the words of the Champion. This announcement was greeted with prolonged cheers from the packed hall and balcony.

'Mr. Sullivan then retired to his dressing room and "Nune" Wallace and Charlie Williams took to the gloves. The fight was sharp and keen, but Nune had no chance against an opponent who was quick and nifty on his feet. Sam Blackrock and "Tricky" Hook followed them into the ring and while Sam was a cool customer, "Tricky" soon warmed his ears. Mr. Gallagher then introduced Harry S. Phillips and the backer of this slugger who stated that he was prepared to match him with anyone in the world to the sum of a shilling to $10,000. Mr. Phillips then bowed in acknowledgement. Sullivan and Mr. Jack Ashton then appeared in costume, the former in his boxing robe, and it was then that many left their seats to rush the platform, eager to shake the Champion's hand. The Champion looked a great man, though slightly fleshy, and his limbs a trifle light; undoubtedly, when in form he must be a crusher! His jaws were quite heavy but nothing out of the way. At present, he is fifteen and one half stones weight; but when at work he would be taken at no more than twelve; he is so quick.

'Four rounds were fought by the Champion and Ashton, who is known as a "squeezer". It is needless to say that John L. could have wiped the floor with his friend; but it must also be said that Mr. Ashton through science and good work showed he is a past master of the game and the crowd warmed to his skill. Several times though Sullivan refrained from hitting when it was apparent that he could have removed his opponent over the ropes and into the crowd. However, the Champion was not minded to deliver the ending that the crowd wished for. The performance then ended with all in the venue most pleased with the performance. After Saturday's exhibition, the lovers of sport in Belfast will be well pleased; and indeed Mr. Sullivan and his entourage will be fully aware that the lovers of sport in the city can appreciate a good thing. During the evening, Mr. Edgar Haine's Orchestra gave a fine performance which added to the evening's enjoyment. Mr. Sullivan and his troupe, we understand, were afterwards entertained in the Queen's Hotel and, at ten o'clock left Belfast for Glasgow by steamer.'

(*Belfast Telegraph*, 19 December 1887)

PETER MAHER AT THE LEINSTER HALL

Galway-born Peter Maher (1869-1940) made his name in Ireland by winning the national middleweight title in 1888, and followed that achievement by taking the heavyweight title in 1890. With his credentials as a world-title contender now enhanced, Maher embarked on a tour of Ireland and his appearance in Dublin's Leinster Hall on 23 August 1895 attracted an audience 'twice the number than the hall was ever designed to hold'. Crowds in the arena climbed into an already crowded balcony, which visibly wilted under the weight of numbers. One of the warm-up bouts saw 'two tall fellows, Ford and Clarke, beat each other with all the vigour of a Dutch housewife cleaning a carpet'.

During another contest between two soldiers, the crowd spilled into the reserved enclosure and the police were powerless as a serious crush ensued. As unofficial fisticuffs broke out amid the chaos in the crowd, the appearance of Maher in the ring was greeted by a massive roar that quelled the unrest to some extent. Maher's agent announced to the crowd that a fee of £25 would be payable to any man who could survive four rounds with the champion. Immediately, a 'giant of a man from London' named Hudson stepped forward to take up the challenge. The fight lasted merely forty seconds until the Englishman was sent crashing to the canvas. Since nobody else came forward to take up the challenge, Maher boxed a tame exhibition against his coach, Mr Lowry.

Maher claimed the world heavyweight crown on 11 November 1895 when he beat the Cork-born Australian Steve O'Donnell in New York. He lost that title to Bob Fitzsimons three months later and his career thereafter was blighted by his lack of boxing finesse and an acute inability to ship a punch. On retirement, he became a well-known bartender in Philadelphia and died in Baltimore in 1940.

2

THE 1900s AND 1910s

JEM ROCHE GOES DOWN WITHOUT A FIGHT

On St Patrick's Day 1908, Ireland awoke to celebrate the country's saint with the anticipation of a sporting extravaganza in the air. That evening, at Dublin's Theatre Royal, Wexford's Jem (James) Roche would meet Canada's Tommy Burns for the world heavyweight title. Born Noah Brusso in Ontario in 1881, the Canadian adopted the name Tommy Burns after he had put an opponent, Ben O'Grady, into a coma and a warrant had been issued for his arrest. He won the world title in 1906, beating 'The Fightin' Kentuckian' Marvin Hart and had defended it on several occasions by the time he arrived in Ireland to face Roche. Jem Roche, a blacksmith by trade, had become the heavyweight champion of Ireland in 1905, when he had stopped 'Young' John L. Sullivan in the twentieth round of their contest in front of a record crowd at the Earlsfort Terrace Rink. Hopes were high – in Ireland anyway – that the Wexford man would bring sporting glory to Ireland on the feast of glorious St Patrick.

From early afternoon, many thousands thronged the streets around the Theatre Royal, hoping to catch a glimpse of both boxers. Burns stood merely 5ft 8in, and remains the smallest man ever to hold the world heavyweight title. By the time the fight commenced, a crowd of 3,500 (no doubt well 'refreshed' from a day's celebrating) had crammed into the arena, expecting a 'ding-dong' battle. The prize at stake was a purse of 1,500 sovereigns; 80 per cent was to go to the winner. Roche was piped into the ring to the sound of 'The Boys of Wexford', while Burns followed to the tune of 'Yankee Doodle'. By the time the preliminaries were completed, it was 10.15 p.m., but the crowd had merely eighty-eight seconds to wait for the spectacular demise of Roche. From the opening bell, Burns waited for his chance and, on taking a 'gentle tap' to the chin from Roche, he responded with a cracking right hook to Roche's jaw that left him face down on the canvas. He was counted out as the thousands outside remained blissfully unaware that the fight had even begun. It is said that one astute spectator, showing great presence of mind, ran panting and dishevelled to the front door of the theatre exclaiming, 'It's terrible, it's terrible! Roche is destroying him and I cannot watch it anymore! I am prepared to sell my ticket for 20 shillings to the first man to hand me the money.' There was no shortage of takers and dozens fought to hand over their shillings for the prized ticket. With the transaction completed, the trickster vanished with great haste into the crowd.

Roche would hold the Irish heavyweight crown until August 1910 when he lost to Matthew Curran at the Empire Theatre. After trying his hand as a promoter, bookmaker and publican he died in his native Wexford in November 1934. Burns' hold on the world title ended on 26 December 1908 in Sydney, Australia, when he lost to Jack Johnson in the fourteenth round of their bout.

CHAMPION BOXER AND HIS WIFE

Sam Young, former middleweight champion of Ireland, had the unenviable task of defending a charge of neglecting his wife in a Belfast police court in January 1909. Claiming that Young had left his wife five months previously, Mr Liddell, representing Mrs Young, claimed that the boxer had earned £4 as the proceeds of a fight a week prior to the case and 'never came to give her a penny'. Admitting that he had neglected his wife, Young offered to find her a home. The magistrate, Mr Wall QC, adjourned the case on the understanding that Mr and Mrs Young 'would find a quiet settlement outside the court'.

YOUNG TAKES IRISH TITLE BY BEATING SULLIVAN

Dublin's Antient Concert Rooms, which were situated at 52 Great Brunswick Street (now Pearse Street), was the location for many professional boxing bills in the early part of the twentieth century. On Monday 5 June 1911, the venue played host the battle for the middleweight championship of Ireland between Dublin's Jim Young and the Irish-American 'Young' John L. Sullivan. The fight, which was for a stake of £200, attracted a healthy crowd, especially in the cheaper seats of the arena. The contest was over twenty rounds and saw both boxers in the ascendancy at various stages, but it turned in Young's favour went he sent Sullivan through the ropes in the eighteenth round and face first onto the floor. It had been Sullivan's fourth attempt to claim the Irish title, having lost three times previously to Wexford's Jem Roche.

BOXING IN OMAGH GOES AHEAD DESPITE OPPOSITION

Professional boxing made its debut in the County Tyrone town of Omagh on St Patrick's evening in 1916, despite opposition from local nationalists. The decision of the Urban Council to lease the Town Hall for the boxing bill prompted the local secretary of the Gaelic League, Mr Joseph Devlin, to write a strongly worded letter of protest to the Town Clerk. Stating that 'the sport of boxing was not the way to celebrate the feast of the National Apostle', Devlin requested that the tournament be cancelled and the promoter be issued with a caution. The letter was read out to the members of the council, but, after discussion, no action was taken. The bouts duly went ahead in front of a hall overflowing with spectators. The crowds were well entertained as they witnessed Omagh's Tommy McGowan's fifteen-round victory over Derry's Bert McIntyre for the top prize of £10.

3

THE 1920s AND 1930s

'COTTER' BROGAN ANGERS THE CLONMEL FAITHFUL

Dubliner Herbert 'Cotter' Brogan made a name for himself in the Irish professional ranks in the 1920s. Brogan joined the army in 1911 and became popular at military tournaments, known for his style and powerful punching. His reputation was enhanced by impressive displays in bouts in England and France during the Great War. He was highly decorated in military terms during that period and returned to Ireland to try his hand in the professional game. He was, however, a boxer who could be somewhat crude in his tactics in the ring. In October 1921, Cotter travelled to the Oisin Theatre in Clonmel, County Tipperary, to face Waterford's Young Jackson in a bantamweight bout. In the fourth round, Jackson complained to the referee that Brogan was 'hitting low'. However, the official refused to intervene, prompting Jackson to leave the ring in protest. As Brogan stood alone amid an increasingly disgruntled crowd, a riot situation began to brew as missiles rained down on to the canvas. Eventually, Jackson restored a semblance of order by returning and the fight recommenced to what were described as 'some lively exchanges'. An irritated Jackson proceeded to knock Brogan to the floor twice and, as the fight neared its end, the Dubliner resorted again to hitting below the belt. Eventually, the referee had seen enough and disqualified Brogan as the crowd screamed for the blood of the Dubliner. In the main bouts that evening, Kid Doyle of Dublin lost out to the local favourite Jack Carroll, while the Clonmel featherweight, Young Smith, beat Peter Cullen of Dublin on points.

MIKE MCTIGUE BEATS
BATTLING SIKI AT SCALA THEATRE

Even the madness that prevailed on the streets of Dublin during the Civil War could not prevent the city coming to a standstill as County Clare's Mike McTigue squared up to the world light-heavyweight champion 'Battling Siki' from Senegal at the Scala Theatre on St Patrick's night in 1923. Michael Francis McTigue had been born into a family of twelve brothers and one sister in Kilnamona, near Ennis, on 26 November 1892. He emigrated from Ireland in 1908 and made a name for himself in both the United States and England before securing a match with Siki in Dublin. The money for the fight had been put up by a syndicate of Irish racehorse owners, led by promoter Tom Singleton. For the fledgling government of the Irish Free State, the hosting of the fight in Dublin conferred international legitimacy on the new political arrangements whilst chaos reigned throughout the country.

Siki had taken the title from George Carpentier in Paris in September 1922 and this, his first defence, was lucrative and seemingly straightforward. Siki's arrival by boat had attracted thousands of spectators to Kingstown, County Dublin. He stayed outside the city at the Claremont Hotel in Howth, where armed guards kept careful watch. He was six years younger than McTigue and partaking in his 117th fight, but the Irish challenger was considered a veteran and not fancied to go the full twenty rounds. Given the ongoing civil unrest throughout Dublin, the arena was by no means full as both boxers entered the ring, while thousands packed the streets to await news of the result. The fight itself was poor with mauling and wild swings the order of the day. Eventually, McTigue began to assert himself and, by the last round, excitement had reached fever pitch. There was now a distinct prospect of an Irish upset in the Dublin air. At the final bell, McTigue was declared the winner and unbridled enthusiasm erupted in the arena and in the surrounding streets. The joyous glee was soon interrupted as the deadening sound of a distant explosion dampened the enthusiasm and the military moved in to clear the streets.

With the world title now secure, McTigue returned to the United States to make his fortune and defended it two times against the 'Phantom of Philly', Tommy Loughran. It was then the rule that a champion had to be stopped during a fight to lose his title. When both fights with Loughran went the distance, McTigue was considered lucky to remain champion. In October 1923, McTigue defended his title in Ohio against Young Stribling in a fight that was declared a draw. McTigue would later claim that he was forced at gunpoint by the promoter to enter the ring that night. McTigue was suspended from boxing in 1924 for refusing to defend his title against Gene Tunney. His tentative hold on the world crown ended at Yankee Stadium on 30 May 1925, when he lost to the youthful Paul Berlenbach. McTigue died in August 1966, having enjoyed a career that lasted from 1914 to 1930. He fought on 141 occasions, winning 81, losing 24, with 36 'no decisions'.

PROFESSIONAL BOXING AT CROKE PARK

Promoter Jim Rice's attractive bill at Croke Park on 21 July 1923 drew a crowd of 11,000 to the north Dublin venue. The chief contest was the bout featuring Ballymena's Pat McAllister and Lancashire's Jack Walden. Known as 'The Irish Terror', McAllister stopped his opponent in the sixth round after Walden had been 'slammed' painfully into the ropes. That bout was followed by the Irish lightweight title fight between Jack Delaney and Pat McCarthy, which Delaney won easily within two rounds. Waterford's 'Battling' Brannigan, who was born Gerald Hurley in Chicago in 1901, was considered to have been an unlucky loser to Tommy Maloney of Dublin. Brannigan was, by 1926, being promoted as 'Dublin's Most Promising Boy' and took Irish titles in the lightweight and middleweight divisions. As a youth, he was taught to sing professionally and turned down an opportunity to join the choir at the Westminster Cathedral. His other claim to fame is that he posed for designer Jerome Connor as the Angel of Peace, which adorns the Lusitania Memorial in Cobh, County Cork. Brannigan's boxing career continued into the 1930s and afterwards he became a renowned boxing coach at St Columba's College in Dublin.

FIRE IN THE ULSTER HALL – BUT FIGHT CONTINUES!

The star attraction at the Ulster Hall in Belfast on Wednesday 29 February 1928 was the appearance – in a refereeing capacity – of the former world flyweight champion, Wales' Jimmy Wilde. The 'Mighty Atom', who had held the world title from 1916 until 1923, was afforded a warm reception by the Belfast fans as he entered the ring to officiate. The main contest of the evening saw the lightweight champion of Ireland, Willie Gilmore, defend his title against the former holder, Kenny Webb. With the champion slightly ahead, an extraordinary scene occurred in the ninth round when a fire broke out on the wooden stage overlooking the ring. As hordes of fans rushed to the doors in panic, the fight was stopped as buckets of water were used to extinguish the flames. As the capacity crowd returned to their seats, the fight recommenced in a haze of acrid smoke. Undeterred, Gilmore boxed on to take the decision on what could have been a night of catastrophe.

PARIS OLYMPIC GAMES 1924

Ireland made its debut in the sport of boxing at the 1924 Olympic Games in Paris. The team of seven, five of which were army representatives, was unsuccessful, but in the welterweight division Sergeant Paddy O'Dwyer lost out for the bronze medal when he was beaten in 'box-off' by Canada's Douglas Lewis (only one bronze medal was awarded to Olympic boxing semi-finalists until 1956). O'Dwyer had won his opening three fights before losing to Argentina's Hector Mendez in the semi-final. In the middleweight class, Garda Jim 'Boy' Murphy lost on a disputed decision to Canada's Les Black. Murphy was a former soldier who joined the Gardaí in 1926 and won national boxing titles in 1924 at middleweight and the light-heavyweight title from 1927 to 1930 and again in 1932. Tancey Lee, coach of the Irish Army, managed the team. The highlight of the squad's tour was a visit to the Place de l'Étoile (now Place Charles de Gaulle) where a harp made from red roses was laid at the Tomb of the Unknown Soldier.

Flyweight	Myles McDonagh
Bantamweight	Bob Hilliard
Featherweight	Mossy Doyle
Lightweight	James Kelleher
Welterweight	Paddy O'Dwyer
Middleweight	Jim Murphy
Light-heavyweight	John Kidley

AMSTERDAM OLYMPIC GAMES 1928

The official trials for places on the Irish team for the Amsterdam Olympic Games took place in an international against Denmark at Dalymount Park on 16 June. A crowd of 8,000 gathered to see Ireland win seven of the eight bouts, with a draw declared in the heavyweight clash between Garda Matthew Flanagan and Neils Andreason. The Irish Olympic Council was dogged by financial difficulties and received a further setback when the Stormont government rejected a request for financial assistance for the boxers. Such were the financial difficulties that two of the Irish competitors paraded in the opening ceremony without official blazers.

In the second series of flyweight class, Belfast's Myles McDonagh lost to the Netherland's 16-year-old Barend Bril. However, Frankie Traynor of the St Paul's club in Dublin won his first three fights, only to lose to eventual gold medallist, Italy's Vittorio Tamagnini, in the bantamweight semi-final. In the box-off for the bronze medal, Traynor was considered unlucky to lose to South Africa's Harry Isaacs. Interestingly, Tamagnini, in his quarterfinal, had beaten Belfast's Jack Garland, a member of the Gordon Highlanders, who was representing Great Britain. Garland turned professional in 1929 and was soon a regular in Irish rings. He won the Irish featherweight title in April 1930 when he beat Frank McAloran in Belfast and retired six years later.

Flyweight	Myles McDonagh
Bantamweight	Frankie Traynor
Featherweight	George Kelly
Lightweight	Willie O'Shea
Welterweight	Patrick Joseph Lenehan
Middleweight	Jack Chase
Light-heavyweight	Jim Murphy
Heavyweight	Matt Flanagan

IRISH GUARDS PACK A PUNCH IN PARIS

An Irish Civic Guards team containing three Olympians acquitted itself in fine style by beating the Paris Police 5-1 in an international tournament at the Salle Wagram in Paris on 26 October 1928. The large crowd present witnessed wins for Frank Cooper, Jack Chase, Jim Murphy and Matt Flanagan for the Irish side, while Jack Forde lost out to Maurice Forgeon in the middleweight bout. At light-heavyweight, Jim Murphy, was awarded the decision when his opponent, Jean Tholey, was disqualified in the second round for a foul blow. The tournament was watched by many dignitaries from the Paris, London and Dublin police, while, bizarrely, the fights took place to the accompaniment of the Paris Police Band.

PRIMO CARNERA VISITS IRELAND

The visit to Ireland of the Italian giant Primo Carnera for two exhibition bouts in June 1932 captured the imagination of the boxing public in both Belfast and Dublin. Carnera, who stood at almost 6ft 7in, was, at the time, the main contender for Max Schmeling's world heavyweight title. His appearances in Belfast's Windsor Park and Dublin's Dalymount Park drew a total attendance of almost 50,000 spectators. Nicknamed the 'Ambling Alp', Carnera was accompanied to the ring in Dublin by the Irish Army Band and thrilled the crowd with a display of speed and accuracy that belied his massive physique. In Belfast the following evening, the Italian almost knocked out his sparring partner, Cyril Woods of Plymouth, with a stray punch that drew gasps from the crowd. Carnera would go on to win the world title by defeating Jack Sharkey in New York in June 1933, only to lose it a year later to Max Baer. That contest, in front of 52,000 fans, saw Carnera knocked to the canvas on eleven occasions and was to signal the waning of the boxing career of a man known also as the 'Walking Mountain'. He retired penniless from boxing in 1946, but later reinvented himself as a professional wrestler, making a small fortune in the process. He died in his home village of Sequals, Italy, aged 60, in June 1967.

JIM MURPHY'S BAD LUCK – LOS ANGELES OLYMPIC GAMES 1932

Political skulduggery intruded on the preparations for the Irish boxing team prior to its departure to Los Angeles. Ireland's top middleweight, Jim Magill of the Royal Ulster Constabulary, was chosen after he had outpointed Garda Jack Chase in an official box-off in February that year. Magill, nonetheless, was prevented from travelling when the Ulster Council of the Irish Amateur Boxing Association (IABA) refused to endorse his selection. The accepted wisdom was that Council was informed by the Stormont government that it would be 'inappropriate' for a member of the RUC to compete under the Irish tricolour representing the Irish Free State, despite the fact that Magill was a seasoned Irish international. The Irish boxers, accompanied by the Garda Commissioner and future leader of the Blueshirts, General Eoin O'Duffy, set sail from Cork in early July. Appearing in his third successive games, Jim Murphy won his quarterfinal against local favourite John Milner. However, Murphy was to sustain serious cuts above both eyes during that fight and entered the ring for his semi-final against Italy's Gino Rossi sporting large plasters. Murphy lasted just over a minute until he was bloodied and forced to retire. Sadly, the injuries to his eyes prevented him from competing in the box-off for the bronze medal.

Bantamweight	Paddy Hughes
Featherweight	Ernie Smith
Welterweight	Larry Flood
Light-heavyweight	Jim Murphy

JACK DOYLE – THE MAN WHO HAD IT ALL

Jack Doyle, nicknamed 'The Gorgeous Gael', led a life that was full to the extreme. He was a boxer, a wrestler, a showman, a singer, an actor, a drinker and a playboy of note. He went from rags to riches and world fame, but died in absolute poverty in London in 1978. Born Joseph Alphonsus Doyle in Cobh, County Cork, in 1913, he had reached 6ft 5in in height by his teenage years. At 17, he assumed the name Jack and joined the Irish Guards, where he excelled in the ring with his somewhat awkward style of boxing. On turning professional, he won his first ten fights, all by knockout, and was matched with Cardiff's Jack Petersen for the British heavyweight title in 1933, aged merely 19. That fight, which took place on 12 July, attracted 70,000 spectators to London's White City as Ireland came to a standstill to listen in on the radio. Both men received £5,000 for their endeavours, but the fight was a total fiasco. Doyle, who was 2 stone heavier than the Welshman, went gung-ho for a knockout. However, in his desperate attempts to land the telling punch, Doyle caught Petersen with four low blows and was duly disqualified. He was subsequently banned from boxing for six months with his purse withheld by the boxing authorities.

Doyle's career had begun to wane by his mid-20s. However, by then he was reputably earning £600 a week on the stage as an Irish crooner. He tried his luck in the United States and lived the high life in Hollywood. Ever-present at society parties, his charm and good looks saw him land starring role in two films, *McGlusky the Sea Rover* in 1934, and *Navy Spy* in 1937. His boxing career trundled on and, on one less than auspicious outing, in 1938, Doyle succeeded in knocking himself out in a fight against Eddie Phillips at the Harringay Arena. With a characteristic wild and inaccurate swing, Doyle lost his balance and his 16-stone frame crashed through the ropes onto the floor, where he lay unconscious for many minutes – it was later claimed that he had 'thrown' the fight.

Tired of life in America, Doyle left his second wife Judith Allen and returned to Ireland in the early 1940s with his new girlfriend, the aristocratic Mexican actress Maria 'Movita' Castaneda. They married at Dublin's Westland Row church, where thousands turned up outside to catch a glimpse of the happy couple. He was by then battling alcoholism and his career was in terminal decline. He made his last appearance in the ring at Dalymount Park in 1943, knocking out Butcher Howell. His problems were exacerbated when Movita lost patience with him and moved back to Hollywood, where she married Marlon Brando. Thereafter, it was all downhill for Doyle. Bankruptcy, a spell in Mountjoy Prison for assaulting a Garda detective, and the demon drink all took their devastating toll. He moved to London and lived a modest lifestyle amid his diminishing legacy. In 1966, he was fined £5 for stealing two blocks of cheese. He died in London on 13 December 1978. His last week had been spent in the back of an abandoned van where he drank cheap wine and beer.

In poverty and death, he was bound for a pauper's grave. Thankfully, the people of Cobh and the ex-Irish Boxers' Mutual Benefit Association intervened and his body was returned to Cobh where many hundreds attended his funeral in the Old Church Cemetery on 22 December. At 55, Jack Doyle had succumbed to alcoholism after a life spent, as he would recall, on 'slow horses and fast women'. A humble man from County Cork had for all too short a period captivated Ireland and beyond. For a boxer who had once three chauffeurs, twenty-five Savile Row suits and dined on caviar washed down with the finest champagne, it was a very sad ending.

BERLIN OLYMPIC GAMES – IRELAND SUSPENDED

The uneasy bedfellows of politics and sport came to the fore again before the 1936 Olympic Games in Berlin. Ireland's status as a partitioned island led to the International Amateur Athletic Federation (IAAF) decreeing at its 1934 Stockholm Conference that all competing Olympic countries must be chosen from within recognised political boundaries. When the Irish National Athletics and Cycling Association failed to give official recognition to the newly formed Northern Ireland Athletic Association, which was affiliated to the governing athletics body in Great Britain, the Olympic Association suspended the Irish Free State in 1935 from international competition. The Irish Olympic Committee forwarded a motion to the Olympic Committee which stated that it would not send a team to Berlin other than a thirty-two-county one. This resolution was disregarded and Ireland remained suspended from competition and was not represented at the Berlin games.

JIM MAGILL – A VICTIM OF SPORTING POLITICS

Jim Magill was a brilliant boxer who represented the Royal Ulster Constabulary and Ireland at international level between 1928 and 1938. He won three British ABA titles at two weights, middleweight in 1934 and 1935 and light-heavyweight 1936. He was selected to represent

Ireland at the Los Angeles Games in 1932, but was prevented from attending by the Ulster Boxing Council. In 1936, he was selected by Britain for the Berlin Olympics, but the IABA vetoed his attendance. His career was trophy-laden. He was Ulster champion on five occasions, a four-time Irish champion, three-time ABA champion and three-time European Police Champion. He was the most outstanding Irish boxer of his generation and the younger brother Davy Magill, Irish professional light-heavyweight and heavyweight champion in the 1920s.

IRELAND'S MONEY WOES – EUROPEAN CHAMPIONSHIPS 1937

At a meeting of the Irish Amateur Boxing Association on 4 March 1937, it was decided that a team would not be sent to represent Ireland at the European Championships in Milan in June that year. Father John McLaughlin, honorary treasurer, reported that the estimated cost for the trip would be £140, but that a further £150 would be required for accommodation and subsistence. With the trials for the championships due to take place on 15 April, Father McLauhghlin forecast that the profit raised at that bill would only be in the region of £60. There was little or no funds to spare and the only course of action open to the IABA was to request that the four provincial councils would agree to make up the deficit. Somewhat predictably, Ireland was notable by its absence from the championships in Milan that year.

JIMMY WARNOCK BEATS BENNY LYNCH AMID GLASGOW CHAOS

The non-title fight between Belfast's Jimmy Warnock and world flyweight champion Benny Lynch drew a crowd of 25,000 to Glasgow's Celtic Park on 2 June 1937. The fight was a rematch as Warnock had defeated Lynch in Belfast's King's Hall some fifteen months previously. Nevertheless, the British Boxing Board of Control refused to sanction the second fight as a clash for Lynch's world title. However, adding spice to the occasion was the fact that Benny Lynch was the darling of the Gorbals and had a loyal Catholic following. Warnock, the Irish champion, was from the 'mean abode' of the Shankill Road, the beating heart of loyalist Belfast. The Shankill Road man had taken a large group of supporters to Scotland and, supplemented by local Glasgow Rangers fans, the atmosphere in the ground was fraught to say the least.

In a constant downpour, the two men went at each other with passion under a black Glasgow sky. Despite being sent to the canvas in the first round, Warnock regained his composure to take the verdict. That was when the trouble began. As Warnock was ushered from the ring surrounded by police, a hail of bottles rained down as hundreds of Lynch's fans 'in the cheaper seats' stormed the inner circle. For a full half hour, the Glasgow fans stood yelling and waving their arms in protest at the decision. Interestingly, while the Irish papers reported the crowd disorder in all its gory detail, the *Glasgow Herald* would only refer to the 'mixed reaction' that greeted Warnock's victory.

Despite the win, Warnock was not offered a crack at Lynch's world crown and had to content himself with an eliminator for his British title against Liverpool's Peter Kane. That fight in August 1937 at Anfield, the home of Liverpool Football Club, was to prove to be Warnock's undoing as he was 'battered all over the ring' in front of 40,000 spectators. Kane subsequently lost to Lynch for his British title. Warnock was from a thoroughbred boxing family and three of his relatives, Billy, Fred and Dave, were all professional fighters between the 1920s and 1950s. Jimmy's career never again hit the heights it achieved that night in Celtic Park and he retired in 1948. He died in 1987 and his funeral on the Shankill Road was one of the biggest-ever witnessed in that part of the city. There is a mural dedicated to Jimmy Warnock in Belfast's Hopewell Crescent.

'SATAN' FLYNN AND CORK'S PADDY ROCHE

A bill featuring a clash between Lefty 'Satan' Flynn and Cork's Paddy Roche attracted a crowd of 7,000 to the National Sporting Club at London's Earl's Court on Monday 9 January 1939. Despite his surname, 'Satan' Flynn was not Irish, but a born-again Christian from the West Indies whose real name was Selvin Campbell. The welterweight fight went the full eight rounds after which an assured Flynn was awarded the verdict on points. His persistency won the day against an opponent who was crude but evasive in the ring. Roche's defeat signalled the beginning of a nine-bout losing streak for the Irishman, during which he was to lose twice again to Flynn, both by knockouts. However, the Cork man's poor run ended in December 1939 when he defeat Mossy Condon over fifteen rounds at the Savoy Theatre in Cork to take the Irish middleweight title.

NATIONAL STADIUM OPENS

The opening of the National Stadium in Dublin on Wednesday 1 March 1939 was marked by great pomp and circumstance, with South Circular Road thronged with spectators hoping to catch a glimpse of the cream of Dublin society. The chief guest on the night was the Minister for Defence, Mr Frank Aiken TD. His speech paid tribute to the role that boxing played in Irish society and he said that, 'It is with no little pride that Irishmen will show foreign visitors this splendid building.' Pointing out that Irishmen had won 568 of their 981 international amateur bouts, Aiken took pride in reminding the crowds that the site of the National Stadium had been derelict just a year previously and congratulated those 'from every part of Ireland whose generosity, brains, skill and hard work had contributed to the completion of the building'. The spectators in the arena that night were then treated to a display of physical fitness by soldiers and four juvenile bouts helped to christen the new ring. For the record, the results were as follows: S. Pringle (St Andrew's) beat H. Lynch (Unity); J. Roe (Tramways) beat F. Duffy (Portobello); R. Byrne (St Vincent's) beat E. Byrne (Sandymount) and T. Christie (Arbour Hill) beat N. Mahon (Catholic Scouts).

The National Stadium, which had a capacity of 2,400 (together with ninety-eight seats in the Members' Gallery), was built for the hosting in Dublin of the 1939 European Championships. It was located on 25,000 square feet of land adjacent to the Griffiths Barracks, which was leased to the IABA by the government. The arena was based on the art deco Liverpool Stadium and contained the most up-to-date showering and changing facilities, together with the novelty of running water at ringside. It was constructed of reinforced concrete and spectators were afforded an uninterrupted view from all parts of the arena. Novelties for fans included an electric scoreboard which displayed the round numbers as the fights progressed.

THE DEATH OF TOM KELLY

On Monday 3 April 1939, 26-year-old Tom Kelly was tragically killed in a work accident at the Tramways bus depot, where he had been employed as a shunter. Kelly had won the Irish senior lightweight title in 1931, beating Private Larry Flood of the army, and was runner-up in the championships on three occasions. A four-time champion of Leinster, Kelly represented Ireland on five occasions, the most notable being at the King's Hall in Belfast in 1936 when he defeated Nazi

Germany's Willi Dixkes in front of a crowd of 5,000 people. Kelly had boxed for the St Tarcisius and Corinthians clubs with distinction and was tipped to be included in the Irish team bound for the USA later that year. In his final two bouts, just weeks before his death, he had defeated both the Ulster and Connacht champions. He was killed by a reversing bus and died on his way to hospital in what the coroner described as an 'absolute tragedy'. His funeral was marked by a large attendance led by the band of the Dublin Tramways Company and a guard of honour of boxers and officials from the Corinthians club. Thomas's widow Margaret and his four children, Monica, John, Thomas and James, led the mourners.

EUROPEAN CHAMPIONSHIP FINALS 1939

The finals of the European Championships took place in the National Stadium on 23 April 1939 and saw Ireland pick up two of the titles. The championships, which had attracted seventy-one competitors from twelve countries, had begun in style a week earlier. At the opening ceremony, the Irish crowd had reserved its warmest welcomes for the visiting teams from Nazi Germany and Great Britain. Notably, sustained applause resounded around the arena as the opening strains of 'God Save the King' rang out in the arena to welcome the British boxers.

On finals night, Jimmy Ingle beat the German Nikolaus Obermaier with a fine display of crisp punching in the flyweight division. However, two days previously, Ingle's quarterfinal 'defeat' to the Italian Giovanni Nardecchia had been greeted with complete uproar in the arena. After an initial silence from the stunned spectators, pandemonium broke out in the stadium. Prolonged choruses of booing, hissing and shouts of rage shook the National Stadium and the uproar continued throughout the next two contests. Finally, with a riot brewing, it was announced that the official Jury d'Appel had reversed the verdict against Ingle which they stated 'was in blatant contradiction to the course of the contest'.

Ireland added a second gold medal on the night when Paddy Dowdall caused a sensation in the featherweight final by defeating the hot favourite, Antoni Czortek of Poland. In the third round, Dowdall carried the fight to his opponent, hitting more cleanly to take the decision to a deafening roar from the home fans. Corporal Dowdall went on to acquit himself with honour, representing Europe against the US Golden Gloves champions in May that year. In Chicago, on 12 May, he defeated Roy Lewis for what was deemed an unofficial world amateur title fight in front of 20,000 spectators. Within the space of a year, Dowdall had enjoyed an emphatic rise in amateur boxing circles. In 1938, he had won the army junior title and, at senior level, he had taken Irish, European and unofficial world honours.

All of the European champions in Dublin were presented with their belts by Mr Frank Aiken, Minister for Defence, and a 'sumptuous' banquet was provided later that evening in Clery's Restaurant for the boxers, officials and guests.

IRELAND'S CREDITABLE DRAW IN CHICAGO

Over 35,000 spectators saw Ireland draw five bouts each with the Chicago Catholic Youth Organisation (CYO) at the Soldiers' Field Arena on 20 July 1939. The occasion saw the great and the good of American boxing in attendance, with both Gene Tunney and Joe Louis refereeing a fight during the tournament. The teams were escorted on to the ring under huge spotlights to a tremendous ovation. Bishop Bernard Shiel administered the pledge of sportsmanship and then the crowd stood bareheaded as the Irish and US flags were raised.

The American team led by five bouts to four as the final contest between Ireland's Patrick O'Sullivan and Cornelius Young began. In an epic last round, O'Sullivan stormed home with an outstanding and fearless display of powerful punching to secure a draw for the Irish team. It had been the first time since 1931 that the CYO had failed to win a tournament in Chicago. Ireland's welterweight, Charlie Evenden, was awarded the trophy for outstanding sportsmanship, while Jimmy Ingle won the Boxer of the Tournament award. It was the final outing for the Irish team in their successful US tour and they set sail for Dublin from New York the following day.

4

THE 1940s

LIMERICK GOES WILD FOR 'JOE LOUIS'

In June 1942, the arrival in Limerick of a powerfully built African named Sam Gerauni convinced locals that the world heavyweight champion Joe Louis had arrived in town. After booking into the Railway Hotel, the Belgian Congo native went for a gentle stroll through the streets of the city and soon large crowds began to follow his every move. Scores of well-wishers requested Gerauni's autograph, while young children showed him their boxing skills. It was only when the hotel receptionist, Molly Harnan, explained to the French-speaking Gerauni that the crowd thought that he was the famous 'Brown Bomber' that the penny dropped.

Such was the excitement on the streets of the city that four police officers were posted on the entrance of the hotel to keep the crowds at bay. Even so, some fans forced their way into the lobby and onwards to Gerauni's room where he unsuccessfully tried to convince them that he was not Joe Louis. Sleep was not to come for poor Gerauni as throughout the night large crowds outside chanted, 'We want Joe Louis'. The following morning Gerauni told local journalists that he had never even worn a pair of boxing gloves in his life, adding, 'I work in a bank in Leopoldville in the Belgian Congo and was just on my way home to Brussels for a quiet rest.'

THE REAL JOE LOUIS APPEARS IN COUNTY FERMANAGH

The real Joe Louis did indeed spend some time in Ireland during the Second World War as he toured US bases in Europe to raise morale as part of the war effort. The USA had thousands of men stationed in Castle Archdale, close to Irvinestown, County Fermanagh, and American soldiers were a regular site at boxing shows in the North. In September 1944, some 2,000 soldiers were attending a grand concert at Castle Archdale and, as the army band was halfway through its programme, Joe Louis walked on to the stage as the surprise guest of honour. He was joined by Tommy Farr, the man whom he had beaten in 1937 for the world heavyweight title. After sparring two rounds with Farr, Louis was joined by Jack Doyle and the two men gave a rendition of 'When Irish Eyes Are Smiling'. Afterwards, both Louis and Doyle were mobbed by the crowds and showered with countless gifts.

POLICE ESCORT FOR BELFAST REFEREE

When Belfast referee Andy Smyth held high the hand of Belfast's Tommy Armour after his contest with Dublin favourite John 'Spike' McCormack, the decision was not well received by the partisan home crowd at Tolka Park. Their fight in July 1942 had been a keenly contested ten rounds, which McCormack had shaded towards the end. However, the verdict in Armour's favour was greeted by catcalls and gardaí were forced to escort Smyth from the arena. Bottles flew and there was a possibility that the rest of the bill would be cancelled as scores of locals from the 'cheap enclosure' tried to storm the ring. Relative calm was eventually restored as gardaí waded into the crowd with batons. The contests restarted with large swathes of the arena lying empty and littered with broken chairs. Although a favourite of the Dublin crowds, McCormack was born in Listowel, County Kerry. At all-Ireland football finals, people were amazed to see him wearing both Kerry and Dublin colours on his lapels. If asked, he would reply to anyone who enquired, 'I fight under two flags'.

EAMONN ANDREWS – THE BROADCASTING BOXER

Born in Dublin in 1922, Eamonn Andrews went on to enjoy world fame as the presenter of *This is Your Life*. On leaving Synge Street Christian Brothers' School, he took up work as an insurance clerk, but harboured deep ambitions to become a sports broadcaster. He bombarded Radio Éireann with letters claiming he was a 'boxing expert who had also taken elocution lessons', until he was finally given an audition. When asked to describe a boxing match from his imagination, he impressed the panel so much that he was given a freelance contract and soon became the voice of Irish boxing at the National Stadium.

Andrews' love of boxing had begun as a teenager at the St Andrew's club where he acted as assistant secretary to Paddy Kilcullen. At the 1944 Irish Junior Championships, Andrews fought his way to the semi-finals on Friday 15 March, where he was to meet Seán Killeen of the Corinthians club at 8.45 p.m. that evening. The only problem for Andrews was that he was due to start a live radio broadcast at ringside fifteen minutes later. With the pressure mounting, Andrew's gave an assured display to win his fight on points and, still in his vest and shorts, went off to do his broadcast. With the programme delivered with accustomed professionalism, later that night Eamonn boxed cleverly to beat Private Peter Fitzgerald to take the Irish title. However, officials at RTÉ had been troubled by the turn of events and his Irish boxing career was deemed to be at an end. He would go on to make a name for himself as a flawless commentator on Irish radio and soon his talent was spotted by the BBC in London.

One of his most famous radio broadcasts for BBC radio came live from the Polo Grounds in New York in June 1960, when Andrews was covering the heavyweight clash between Floyd Patterson and Ingmar Johannsen. Always a journalist to try to get a fresh angle on a fight, Andrews astounded his producer by leaving his seat to try to interview Patterson as he was making his way to the ring. Not surprisingly, he was requested by officials to resume his place. It was a prime example of his unquestionable charm and self-belief.

UNRULY CROWDS AT DALYMOUNT PARK

Dublin sports journalist, A.P. MacWeeney, reached the end of his reporting tether when unruly crowds swarmed around the ring at an open-air bill at Dalymount Park on Saturday 19 August 1944. The problems in the grounds arose when spectators flooded the pitch from the terraces to get a better view of the proceedings and deposed of 'some two hundred worthy citizens who were seated in a wide circle around the ring'. The 'worthy citizens' were engulfed by the masses of boys and men who pushed themselves to the ringside, forcing journalists to lift their notebooks to make way. MacWeeney spent the rest of the bill fending off small boys who were trying to climb over him to get a better view. However, the final straw was when a local woman commandeered the press table and began selling chocolates and candy apples, doing a brisk business in the process. 'Short of barbed wire, I do not know how the standing spectators can be kept away from the ring,' suggested MacWeeney. 'If the promoters do not act against this insoluble problem, the future of open-air boxing in Dublin will remain in doubt,' he added.

CUMANN DORNALA TUAISCEART NA CATHRACH – NORTH CITY ABC

There was a novel experience for the Scottish boxing team in October 1945 when they appeared at the National Stadium in the Cumann Dornala Tuaisceart na Cathrach (North City Boxing Club) tournament. Since the event had been hosted by the only Irish-speaking club in the country, the introductions and results were all delivered in Irish. It was the first time that Irish was used at an international boxing tournament. However, if the Scots' boxers were not disorientated enough, they had arrived in Dublin only at 7.30 p.m. that evening, having endured a severe and stormy crossing of the Irish Sea.

ROYAL ULSTER CONSTABULARY (RUC) BOXING CLUB

The RUC's boxing club was founded in 1928 by Captain T.D. Morrison and Tom Rothwell. From then until the 1960s, the RUC was a leading force in Ulster and Irish boxing, both in the ring and in the administration of the sport. Amateur boxing had enjoyed a long association with the police in Ireland, with the Royal Irish Constabulary having laid the foundations for the sport. Boxing was looked upon as important asset in police training; not only as a useful tool for self-defence and self-discipline, but also as a way of engaging with the local community. The first tournament organised by the RUC took place in December 1928 and included boxers from the gardaí boxing team. Over the years, the RUC became the driving force within Ulster boxing and its representatives lifted many Ulster and Irish titles. Among them were Jim Magill, Johnny McNeill and Harry Taylor, who won five successive Ulster titles between 1946 and 1950 and Irish titles in 1946 and 1947. In 1956, Victor Winnington became the last RUC boxer to win Ulster and Irish titles when he won the light-heavyweight titles. Later that year, Canadian-born Winnington represented Ireland at the Melbourne Olympic Games. Others, such as Sam Hayes and Billy Duncan, were well-respected referees who officiated at the Olympic Games in Rome in 1960.

IRELAND'S DECISIVE 7-1 WIN OVER USA

The first appearance by an American international boxing team in Dublin for fifteen years set off a stampede for tickets for the clash with Ireland at the National Stadium on 1 June 1946. Dave Connell got Ireland off to a winning start at flyweight, while in the bantamweight clash, Keith Hamilton took the narrowest of decisions over Ireland's Peter Maguire. Leo Kelley's tendency to hit below the belt saw him disqualified against Ireland's Bertie Coughlan. At light-heavyweight, Constable Harry Taylor fought back after going to the canvas twice in the opening round to record a victory over John Tucker, the Ohio Golden Gloves champion. Taylor's coolness under pressure kept him going until he got the better of the bout midway through the third round, but he was deemed lucky to get the decision. In the heavyweight bout, Gearóid Ó Colmáin was fortunate to win after a stray punch from Charles Lester left the local favourite rolling in agony the canvas. The referee deemed the punch a low blow and duly disqualified the American.

	FLYWEIGHT			
(Ireland)	Dave Connell	*beat*	John Arduini	(USA)
	BANTAMWEIGHT			
(USA)	Keith Hamilton	*beat*	Peter Maguire	(Ireland)
	FEATHERWEIGHT			
(Ireland)	Bertie Coughlan	*beat*	Leo Kelley	(USA)
	LIGHTWEIGHT			
(Ireland)	Paddy Byrne	*beat*	George McGee	(USA)
	WELTERWEIGHT			
(Ireland)	Tom Hyde	*beat*	Roscoe Hinson	(USA)
	MIDDLEWEIGHT			
(Ireland)	Michael McKeon	*beat*	Harold Anspach	(USA)
	LIGHT-HEAVYWEIGHT			
(Ireland)	Harry Taylor	*beat*	John Tucker	(USA)
	HEAVYWEIGHT			
(Ireland)	Gearóid Ó Colmáin	*beat*	Charles Lester (disqualified)	(USA)

STADIUM ERUPTS FOR Ó COLMÁIN'S VICTORY

Ireland again hosted the European Championships in 1947 when 106 competitors from fifteen countries descended on Dublin in May that year. By finals night, Ireland had two boxers going for gold medals. Army boxer Peter Maguire lost out in the featherweight final to Kurt Kreuger of Sweden. Despite putting up a splendid fight, the superior strength and reach of the Swede won him the title over Maguire. The nation then came to a halt as Eamonn Andrews described live on radio the heavyweight final between Dubliner Gearóid Ó Colmáin and George Scriven of Great Britain. Ó Colmáin was the more aggressive throughout the bout and at the final bell there was never any doubt about the result. When the result was announced, the National Stadium erupted in delight and Ó Colmáin was carried shoulder high from the ring in triumph.

In the welterweight final, Irish supporters urged on Great Britain's John Ryan as he battled with France's Charles Humez. The crowd regarded Ryan as one of their own and there were shouts of 'Come on, Ireland' and 'Come on, Tipperary' as he boxed his way to victory. Ireland received many plaudits for its organisation of the championships. The secretary of the International Boxing Board, Lieutenant Colonel R.H. Russell, paid tribute to the sportsmanship of the Dublin fans. He added Dublin was 'a beautiful capital full of capital sportsmen'.

Flyweight	Willie Barnes	(Victory, Belfast)
Bantamweight	Dave Connell	(Avona)
Featherweight	Peter Maguire	(Arbour Hill)
Lightweight	Michael 'Maxie' McCullagh	(Corinthians)
Welterweight	Eddie Cantwell	(Clonmel)
Middleweight	Mick McKeon	(Crumlin)
Light-heavyweight	Jim Corbett	(Glen, Cork)
Heavyweight	Gearóid Ó Colmáin	(North City)

THE PROFESSOR WHO CHOSE EXAMS OVER OLYMPIC BOXING

As a student at University College Dublin, Seamus Timoney won the British Universities Boxing Championships in four successive years during the 1940s. One of his most eye-catching victories, however, came just months before the 1948 London Olympics when he defeated the 'Iron Man' of Irish boxing, Waterford's Peter Crotty. On being offered a place on the Irish Olympic team, Timoney, with his final exams in mechanical engineering approaching, turned down the chance of lifetime. He went on to enjoy a brilliant business and academic career. Seamus was the eldest of a family of ten children. Personal tragedy was to strike the Timoney family in 1950 when Seamus's well-respected father, Lieutenant Colonel Seamus Timoney senior, died in a cycling accident in County Galway.

MICK MCKEON 'ROBBED' – LONDON OLYMPIC GAMES 1948

The political shenanigans over citizenship continued to overshadow Ireland's participation at the Olympic Games. However, by 1948, the country, thanks to Articles 2 and 3 of the 1937 Constitution, had been recognised by the International Olympic Committee as a thirty-two county entity. Given the close proximity of London, Ireland sent over 100 competitors, which included a team of eight boxers. Known as the 'Austerity Games' the boxing took place at the Empire Pool at the Wembley Arena on a temporary platform erected over the swimming pool. That pool this day remains intact underneath the arena floor.

Mick McKeon was Ireland's unluckiest boxer in 1948. Having defeated Canadian and Iranian opponents, he outfought reigning European champion, Aimé Escudie of France, in the quarterfinal. In his semi-final later that day, he lost against England's John Wright, a verdict that Dick Wilkes of the *Irish Press*, described as 'one of the greatest pieces of boxing injustices I have ever seen'. McKeon was then denied a chance of becoming the first Irishman to claim a boxing medal when he was prevented by officials from boxing Ivano Pontana of Italy for third place. Ireland's medical officer advised McKeon that he could not fight since he had aggravated a shoulder injury during that bout. Irish officials were adamant that McKeon's withdrawal was not due to any dissatisfaction over the semi-final verdict. Six of Ireland's eight boxers claimed victories at the London Games, with only Willie Barnes and Kevin Martin being eliminated in the first series of bouts in their respective divisions.

Flyweight	Willie Barnes
Bantamweight	Willie Lenihan
Featherweight	Kevin Martin
Lightweight	Michael 'Maxie' McCullagh
Welterweight	Peter Foran
Middleweight	Mick McKeon
Light-heavyweight	Hugh O'Hagan
Heavyweight	Gearóid Ó Colmáin

RINTY MONAGHAN –
THE 'CROONING CHAMPION'

The name of John Joseph 'Rinty' Monaghan will live long in the annals of Irish sporting greats. Rinty began his boxing career in Clara 'Ma' Copley's famous boxing booths in Belfast and had his first paid fight at the age of 14 in 1932. That taste of professional boxing was to herald the beginnings of a sparkling career that would see Rinty command a huge following in his hometown. A short break for military service during the Second World War interrupted his rise to the top. After the war, the King's Hall became his fortress and he scaled the heights to bring a world crown to his native Belfast. His victory in London over Dado Marino for a share of the National Boxing Association's world title was perhaps the most significant breakthrough in Irish boxing in the twentieth century. It made Monaghan an instant legend in his native Belfast and beyond. On 23 March 1948, at a packed King's Hall, the remarkable flyweight claimed the undisputed world championship when he dispatched the durable Scot Jackie Paterson in the seventh round. As Paterson lay prostrate on the canvas, Rinty jigged in the ring and was soon to lead the crowd in a rendition of 'When Irish Eyes Are Smiling'. Bonfires were lit across Belfast to acknowledge the achievement of a man whose pre-fight diet saw him drink of a cocktail of goat's milk, raw eggs and brandy.

He retired from boxing in 1950 as the holder of the British, European, Empire and world titles after a career which spanned sixty-six professional outings, losing on just eight occasions. His retirement was brought about through poor health, which dogged him for the rest of his days. Notably, the notorious East End gangster Ronnie Kray, in his autobiography recalled, 'When I was 12, I met the great Rinty Monaghan in Jack Solomons' gym and he gave me a shamrock buttonhole, which I still have.' As an entertainer, Rinty thrilled thousands all over Ireland with his band The Rintonians. In 1969, he finally got the recognition he deserved when he was inducted in the Irish Sporting Hall of Fame.

By early 1984, Rinty was a shadow of the man who had thrilled Ireland, but his fame was boundless and he had countless admirers across the world. The 'Crooning Champion' died aged 66 in Belfast on 3 March 1984 and his funeral was attended by thousands from the local boxing fraternity. He had been born into a family of fifteen in 1918 and fought the hard way to become champion of the world. The *Irish News*, in its editorial on the day of his funeral commented, 'The last bell has rung and he has gone to take his place in the hall of champions; the tears will eventually dry, but the memories will live forever.'

MAXIE MCCULLAGH TAKES EUROPEAN GOLD – OSLO 1949

Maxie McCullagh took the lightweight gold medal at the 1949 European Championship in Oslo by outpointing France's Mohammed Ammi. The 24-year-old Mullingar man became the third Irishman to take a gold medal at European level, following in the footsteps of Jimmy Ingle and Gearóid Ó Colmáin. The small Irish contingent in the Bislett Stadium was overjoyed when McCullagh's victory was announced and he was carried shoulder high through the arena to the dressing room. Dave Connell added to Ireland's medal haul when he took bronze in the featherweight competition. However, Mick McKeon, who had been tipped for a gold medal, went out to the Czech, Frantisek Svaro, in the first round of competition.

5

THE 1950s

MILLIGAN SURPRISES CONNELL – NATIONAL SENIOR FINALS 1950

A huge crowd was in attendance at the National Stadium on 18 March for the national senior finals, which provided some tough and skilful boxing. In the featherweight clash, Belfast's Terry Milligan made his mark by defeating the hot favourite, Avona's Dave Connell, on points. Both boxers would later win bronze medals at the 1951 European Championships in Milan and represent Ireland at the Helsinki Olympic Games in 1952. Connell won four senior championships titles between 1946 and 1951, while Milligan would go on to claim six straight Irish titles between 1950 and 1955, claiming a second bronze medal in the European Championships in Warsaw in 1953.

At welterweight, the 'Iron Man', Peter Crotty, put in a superb last round of powerful punching to see-off an assured challenge from Martin Humpston of the St Francis club. Dungarvan man Crotty, who boxed out of the Clonmel club, would claim further welterweight titles in 1951 and 1952 and represented Ireland at the Helsinki Olympic Games in 1952. The winner of the lightweight final, Christopher Foley, came from a well-known family of boxers from Dunshaughlin, County Meath. On one famous day in the 1940s, five Foley brothers, Christopher, Benny, Podger, Joe and Seamus all won bouts at the National Stadium in the juvenile championships.

	FLYWEIGHT			
(St Francis)	Jimmy Henry	*beat*	Charlie Murray	(Sandymount)
	BANTAMWEIGHT			
(Arbour Hill)	Benny Carabini	*beat*	Paddy Kelly	(Sandymount)
	FEATHERWEIGHT			
(Short and Harland)	Terry Milligan	*beat*	Dave Connell	(Avona)

	LIGHTWEIGHT			
(Dunshaughlin)	Christopher Foley	*beat*	Pat Buckley	(Mallow)
	WELTERWEIGHT			
(Clonmel)	Peter Crotty	*beat*	Martin Humpston	(St Francis)
	MIDDLEWEIGHT			
(Crumlin)	Mick McKeon	*beat*	George Lavery	(St Georges)
	LIGHT-HEAVYWEIGHT			
(Crumlin)	Willie Duggan	*beat*	Gerry Dwyer	(Civil Service)
	HEAVYWEIGHT			
(North City)	Gearóid Ó Colmáin	*beat*	Eamonn Walsh	(Garda)

Ó COLMAIN'S EIGHTH TITLE – NATIONAL SENIOR FINALS 1951

Gearóid Ó Colmáin (1924-2008) secured his eighth Irish title (two at light-heavyweight and six at heavyweight) when Kerry man Jim Griffin found the champion's left hooks too much to deal with in the third round of their bout. The most popular win of the night belonged to Drogheda's Tony 'Socks' Byrne, who added the senior title to his junior crown with an assured display against Steve Coffey. Martin Humpston of the St Francis club took the first-ever national light-middleweight title. The runner-up in the bantamweight final, John Kelly of Belfast, turned professional after claiming a silver medal at the European Championships in Milan later that year and would go on to claim the British and European professional titles at the King's Hall in 1953, when he defeated Scotland's Peter Keenan. He held the European crown until February 1954 when Robert Cohen took the title at the same venue.

	FLYWEIGHT			
(Sandymount)	Ando Reddy	*beat*	Cpl Willie O'Brien	(Collins Barracks)
	BANTAMWEIGHT			
(Corinthians)	Paddy Kelty	*beat*	John Kelly	(St George's)
	FEATHERWEIGHT			
(Drogheda)	Tony Byrne	*beat*	Steve Coffey	(Pollikoff's)
	LIGHTWEIGHT			
(Avona)	Dave Connell	*beat*	Maxie McCullagh	(Corinthians)
	LIGHT-WELTERWEIGHT			
(Short and Harland)	Terry Milligan	*beat*	Ollie Byrne	(Guinness)
	WELTERWEIGHT			
(Clonmel)	Peter Crotty	*beat*	Sammy Hamilton	(Windsor Belfast)
	LIGHT-MIDDLEWEIGHT			
(St Francis)	Martin Humpston	*beat*	Seán Killeen	(Corinthians)

	MIDDLEWEIGHT			
(Crumlin)	Mick McKeon	*beat*	Kevin Doyle	(Arbour Hill)

	LIGHT-HEAVYWEIGHT			
(Crumlin)	Willie Duggan	*beat*	Hugh O'Hagan	(Aer Lingus)

	HEAVYWEIGHT			
(North City)	Gearóid Ó Colmáin	*beat*	Seamus Griffin	(Tralee)

THE ITALIAN WHO FORGOT THE RULES

The international match between Ireland and Italy at the National Stadium on 9 November 1951 almost ended in uproar as light-welterweight match between Gerry Arnold and Umberto Vernaglione bordered on the farcical. Under pressure, the Italian resorted to roughhouse tactics, throwing at least three rabbit punches to Arnold's head. In addition, the Italian twice tried to headbutt his Irish opponent and administered several blows to Arnold's back and neck. When Arnold was struck while he was on the canvas, the crowd screamed for the referee to caution the Italian. The referee – himself an Italian with seemingly poor eyesight – refused to intervene. Arnold recovered to take the fight on points as the Italian, amid shaking fists and catcalls, was ushered away from the ring. The international ended level at 5-5 draw, with Gearóid Ó Colmáin securing the draw by beating Giacomo Di Segni in the heavyweight fight. Vernaglione turned professional in his native Italy in 1953 and claimed the national welterweight title in 1957. His career was blighted somewhat by four disqualifications, twice for headbutting.

HARRY PERRY'S PRECOCIOUS TALENT – NATIONAL SENIOR FINALS 1952

John McNally of the White City club had little difficulty securing his first senior title when he stopped Sandymount's Mick Towers in the second round of their bantamweight final. Towers was no pushover, having beaten some of the top boxers in Ireland, but he had no answer for the speed and power of McNally. Towers ('wisely', according to *The Irish Times*) retired before the end of the second round and the cup went north.

At welterweight, Peter Crotty endured a tough struggle and was in difficulties early on against the hard-hitting Ollie Byrne. Durable as ever, Crotty kept battling on regardless and eventually wore down his opponent. The best performance of the night belonged to 17-year-old Terenure College boxer Harry Perry, whose accurate punching kept Tommy Reddy at bay to ensure a fine win. Sadly for Perry, the IABA decreed that he was too young to compete for Ireland at the Helsinki Olympics and opted for

Reddy. Gearóid Ó Colmáin claimed his seventh heavyweight title (to add to his two at light-heavyweight) and duly announced his retirement to a standing ovation. In 1980, he became the first Irish amateur boxer to be inducted into the Texaco Irish Sporting Hall of Fame.

	FLYWEIGHT			
(Sandymount)	Ando Reddy	*beat*	Jim Dowling	(Freshford)
	BANTAMWEIGHT			
(White City)	John McNally	*beat*	Mick Towers	(Sandymount)
	FEATHERWEIGHT			
(Terenure)	Harry Perry	*beat*	Tommy Reddy	(Crumlin)
	LIGHTWEIGHT			
(Drogheda)	Tony Byrne	*beat*	Kevin Martin	(Mount Street)
	LIGHT-WELTERWEIGHT			
(Short and Harland)	Terry Milligan	*beat*	George Arnold	(Avona)
	WELTERWEIGHT			
(Clonmel)	Peter Crotty	*beat*	Ollie Byrne	(Guinness)
	LIGHT-MIDDLEWEIGHT			
(Corinthians)	Fergus Kilmartin	*beat*	John Murphy	(Sandymount)
	MIDDLEWEIGHT			
(Crumlin)	Willie Duggan	*beat*	George Lavery	(St George's)
	CRUISERWEIGHT			
(Nemo, Cork)	Raymond Donnelly	*beat*	Gerry O'Riordan	(Garda)
	HEAVYWEIGHT			
(North City)	Gearóid Ó Colmáin	*beat*	John Nisco	(Trinity College)

IRELAND TAKES SILVER –
HELSINKI OLYMPIC GAMES 1952

Born in Belfast in 1932, John McNally became the first Irish boxer to win an Olympic medal when he took silver in Helsinki in the bantamweight competition in 1952. At the Games, McNally battled his way to the final by winning three bouts, all by unanimous decisions. After his semi-final victory against the Korean, Joon Ho Kang, John stood on the threshold of the Olympic title. However, whilst he had not been tested by Kang, his back had received severe rope burns because of the Belfast man's defensive tactics. On his way back to the changing room, two medics accosted McNally outside the ring to look at his shredded back and immediately ordered him to the dressing room to have the wounds dressed. John, himself, takes up the story:

'When we got to the dressing room, the doctor took out a bottle of pure alcohol and told me to lie face down on a bench, and warned me that the alcohol would sting my back badly,' said John. 'I recall there were two boxers lying meditating on the benches beside me, preparing mentally for their bouts. Both got up and took one of my hands each in preparation for the treatment. To this day, I can feel the pain, and still smell the alcohol on my back. It was terrible. I was about to scream and I squeezed the boxers' hands hard in reaction to the pain. Only later did I come to realise that the men who held my hands that day were Floyd Patterson and Charles Adkins – two legends in the making. It is an act of kindness that I have never forgotten.'

In the final, John was to face the hometown favourite Pentti Hämäläinen. The fight was won by the Finn on a split decision, much to the joy of the home fans. Pentti was cautioned twice for holding and hitting low during a messy affair. The *Daily Telegraph* reporter, Lainson Wood, described the result as 'the last fling of outrageous fortune of the 1952 Olympic Games'. He added that the decision had 'cast its poisoned arrow in the direction of Ireland when John McNally from Belfast was beaten in the final of the bantamweight contest. Hämäläinen, a strong and courageous little Finn, was permitted, without caution, by one of the worst referees of this ill-assorted band, to land swinging punches with his forearms and the heel of his glove,' he added.

McNally kept composed during the medal ceremony and only later did the Irish contingent learn that the 'anthem' lined up on the turntable, should McNally have won, was 'It's a Long Way to Tipperary'. Terry Milligan won his opening two bouts but was beaten by Italy's Bruno Vistilin in his quarterfinal. However, should Milligan have won, he was not guaranteed a bronze medal. The awarding of bronze medals to both beaten semi-finalists was introduced in Melbourne in 1956. Both McNally and Ando Reddy, at 19 years of age, were Ireland's youngest competitors, while Willie Duggan was the nation's oldest boxer at 26.

In 1953, John McNally won a bronze medal at the European Championships held in Warsaw. In June that year, he won his three bouts at the US Golden Gloves Championship in Chicago, where he was representing Europe. He was awarded an honorary pair of Golden Gloves in recognition of that achievement. In November, he was made unofficial bantamweight champion of Germany in recognition of his feat of having defeated that country's three former bantamweight champions in the space of eighteen months.

Flyweight	Ando Reddy
Bantamweight	John McNally
Featherweight	Tommy Reddy
Lightweight	Kevin Martin
Light-welterweight	Terry Milligan
Welterweight	Peter Crotty
Middleweight	Willie Duggan
Heavyweight	John Lyttle

MCNALLY LOSES TO REDDY – NATIONAL SENIOR FINALS 1953

Eight titles changed hands at the National Stadium on 21 March, but the upset of the night saw Ando Reddy take John McNally's title at bantamweight. It was a superb and battling last round finish that swung the bout in Reddy's favour. McNally, the darling boy of Irish boxing, had scored well against his fellow Olympian in the opening two rounds, but could not contain the final onslaught from the man from the Sandymount club in Dublin. In the heavyweight final, Jim Robinson put in a brave performance but was narrowly beaten by reigning champion John Lyttle of the St George's club. In the featherweight decider, Harry Perry retained his title with a win over his great rival Fred Tiedt. Despite losing his title, John McNally retained his place on the Ireland team that would travel to meet Scotland the following week. It was announced that only McNally and Terry Milligan would represent Ireland at the European Championships in Warsaw in May. Both boxers claimed bronze medals.

	FLYWEIGHT			
(Irish Army)	Eddie O'Connor	*beat*	Jimmy Carson	(Star)
	BANTAMWEIGHT			
(Sandymount)	Ando Reddy	*beat*	John McNally	(White City)
	FEATHERWEIGHT			
(Terenure)	Harry Perry	*beat*	Fred Tiedt	(South City)
	LIGHTWEIGHT			
(Arbour Hill)	Steve Coffey	*beat*	Jimmy Brown	(White City)
	LIGHT-WELTERWEIGHT			
(Short and Harland)	Terry Milligan	*beat*	Joe Larkin	(Transport)
	WELTERWEIGHT			
(Crumlin)	Tommy Maguire	*beat*	Eamonn Ryan	(Limerick)
	LIGHT-MIDDLEWEIGHT			
(Monaghan)	Maurice Loughran	*beat*	Mick Docherty	(Robinsons, Belfast)
	MIDDLEWEIGHT			
(White City)	George Lavery	*beat*	Willie Wright	(White City)
	LIGHT-HEAVYWEIGHT			
(Arbour Hill)	Paddy Lyons	*beat*	Mick Fisher	(Ballymore-Eustace)
	HEAVYWEIGHT			
(St George's)	John Lyttle	*beat*	Jim Robinson	(South City)

KELTY STORMS HOME – NATIONAL SENIOR FINALS 1954

The fight of the 1954 championships occurred in the semi-finals when Harry Perry beat Tony Byrne of Drogheda on his way to a victory over Paddy Martin in the lightweight final. One of the closest bouts of finals' night saw Paddy Kelty box his way to a fine victory against Fred Tiedt. Tiedt, who very wisely decided to try to keep Kelty at long range, relying on his fast footwork and stabbing left, was outdone by a storming last round which saw the contest swing in Kelty's favour. There wasn't much to choose between Seán Wright and Johnny Logan, but Wright was the more polished fighter of the two on the night. Tony Myers put in a gallant performance against the compact Belfast flyweight John Matthews, but the northern southpaw's solid body punching gave him a clear advantage.

	FLYWEIGHT			
(St John Bosco)	John Matthews	*beat*	Tony Myers	(Glen, Cork)
	BANTAMWEIGHT			
(Sandymount)	Ando Reddy	*walkover*		
	FEATHERWEIGHT			
(South City)	Paddy Kelty	*beat*	Fred Teidt	(Corinthians)
	LIGHTWEIGHT			
(Terenure)	Harry Perry	*beat*	Paddy Martin	(St Vincent's)
	LIGHT-WELTERWEIGHT			
(Phoenix, Dublin)	Seán Wright	*beat*	Johnny Logan	(St Francis, Limerick)
	WELTERWEIGHT			
(Short and Harland)	Terry Milligan	*beat*	Jimmy McLaughlin	(Sandymount)
	LIGHT-MIDDLEWEIGHT			
(Guinness)	Ollie Byrne	*beat*	John Murphy	(Sandymount)
	MIDDLEWEIGHT			
(Robinsons, Belfast)	Mick Doherty	*beat*	Gerry Henry	(Dealgan)
	LIGHT-HEAVYWEIGHT			
(Arbour Hill)	Paddy Lyons	*beat*	Mick Fisher	(Ballymore-Eustace)
	HEAVYWEIGHT			
(South City)	Jim Robinson	*beat*	Eugene Walsh	(Garda)

'SUGAR' RAY ROBINSON FOR THE PHOENIX PARK?

On 25 June 1952, 'Sugar' Ray Robinson relinquished his world middleweight title to begin a lucrative career in show business. The champion's decision left many boxing fans unhappy as the prospect of a third clash between Sugar Ray and Englishman Randolph Turpin was now on hold. The two had met twice in 1951, when, in July, Turpin took the world title off Robinson in London, only to lose in a rematch three months later. Despite the fact that Robinson had retired, 'Jolly' Jack Solomons tried to secure a third fight between the two men for London in 1953. On being told that he would be limited to an outdoor crowd of 50,000, Solomons made plans to host the fight at the racecourse at the Phoenix Park, where he suggested, 'There is no crowd restriction and only a small percentage of entertainment tax to pay.'

The London promoter planned to stage the fight as part of a race meeting at the park and predicted a crowd of over 100,000 would attend. Unfortunately for Solomons, Robinson chose to stay in retirement until he eventually returned to the ring in 1955, retaining his world title later that year. In the twilight of his career, Robinson, at 44 years of age, lost to Irish-born British middleweight champion Mick Leahy at the Paisley Ice Rink in Scotland. Leahy, who was originally from Cork, but based in Coventry, beat the legend over ten rounds in September 1964. Many pundits felt that Robinson had done enough to earn a draw, since Leahy, it was reported in the *Glasgow Herald*, 'had little but crude aggression on his side'.

MARTIN THORNTON – THE REAL 'QUIET MAN'

In 1951, the arrival in Ireland of John Wayne and Maureen O'Hara to film *The Quiet Man* presented an opportunity for Spiddal-born boxer Martin Thornton to resurrect his boxing skills. A distant cousin of the film's director, John Forde, Thornton had been the inspiration behind Wayne's character, Seán 'Trooper Thorn' Thornton. On meeting Forde, Thornton was offered a part in the film as the stunt double for Victor McLaglen's character 'Squire' Danagher in the famous fight scenes. McLaglen had indeed been a fighter of note who had boxed an exhibition with Jack Johnson in 1909. He and Thornton were to become formidable drinking partners in Cong, County Galway, during the making of the film.

Martin Thornton's previous career in the ring had seen him take the Irish heavyweight title by beating Paddy Sullivan in the Theatre Royal in 1944. His big chance of fame came in August 1945, when he faced the newly crowned British champion, Bruce Woodcock, at the same venue for what was described as a record purse. It was billed as the puncher (Thornton) against the stylist (Woodcock) and over 30,000 people greeted Woodcock on his arrival in Dublin, where he was afforded a civic reception by the Lord Mayor, Peadar S. Doyle. The fight was won easily by Woodcock as he chased Thornton around the ring, catching him with powerful punches. An eye-splitting right hand caught Thornton in the second round, but he fought on courageously, responding with a sharp uppercut to the Englishman's chin. The third round was all action, but a series of combinations closed over Thornton's left eye and his corner sensibly threw in the towel.

The defeat to Woodcock effectively ended Thornton's career and, after his appearances in *The Quiet Man*, he returned to Spiddal to look after the family farm. In later years, he admitted that he had in fact bet on Woodcock to beat him in their fight and had extracted a lucrative purse of £800 from promotor Jack Solomons for his less than auspicious showing. A renowned musician, historian and folklorist, with a taste for the finest poteen, Martin Thornton died aged 67 in 1984.

GILROY INJURED, RAFTER TAKES CROWN – NATION SENIOR FINALS 1955

There were few bouts of real quality at the senior finals on 19 March 1955. The only fight of note occurred in the light-welterweight bout between Harry Perry and his British Railways clubmate John Sweeney. In each of the rounds, Sweeney caught Perry with crisp right hands that shook him momentarily. Perry, though, with his tireless aggression and speed, took the decision, but Sweeney had announced himself as a serious rival to Perry in that weight class. In the flyweight division, Chris Rafter, in the absence of the injured Freddie Gilroy, beat Des Adams with consummate ease to take the title. However, the IABA ordered Rafter and Gilroy to meet in a box-off at the National Stadium on 22 April when Gilroy prevailed and booked himself a place on the Irish team for the European Championships in Berlin.

	FLYWEIGHT			
(North City)	Chris Rafter	*beat*	Des Adams	(St Andrew's)
	BANTAMWEIGHT			
(Star)	Martin Smith	*beat*	Bruce Robertson	(Terenure)
	FEATHERWEIGHT			
(Army)	Private Tommy Butler	*beat*	Eddie Duffy	(Athlone)
	LIGHTWEIGHT			
(Arbour Hill)	Steve Coffey	*beat*	Paddy O'Leary	(Athlone)
	LIGHT-WELTERWEIGHT			
(British Railways)	Harry Perry	*beat*	John Sweeney	(British Railways)
	WELTERWEIGHT			
(Sandymount)	Jimmy McLoughlin	*beat*	Joe Foley	(Dunshaughlin)
	LIGHT-MIDDLEWEIGHT			
(Short and Harland)	Terry Milligan	*beat*	Danny King	(Arbour Hill)
	MIDDLEWEIGHT			
(Arbour Hill)	Peter Burke	*beat*	Gerry Henry	(Dealgan)
	LIGHT-HEAVYWEIGHT			
(Arbour Hill)	Paddy Lyons	*beat*	Bill Chinn	(Dublin University)
	HEAVYWEIGHT			
(South City)	Jim Robinson	*beat*	Tommy Bruce	(Sandymount)

IRELAND HUMBLED –
EUROPEAN CHAMPIONSHIPS BERLIN 1955

The European Championships of 1955 opened on 27 May and Ireland sent a seven-strong team. At flyweight, Freddie Gilroy was expected to claim a medal, while the experienced Ando Reddy was chosen at bantamweight. Eddie Duffy represented Ireland at featherweight, Steve Coffey, a police officer based in Manchester, at lightweight and Harry Perry at light-welterweight, while two Arbour Hill boxers, Peter Burke and Paddy Lyons, were selected at middleweight and light-heavyweight respectively. Despite the high hopes of the Irish management, by the third day of competition, the team of seven had been reduced to two. Harry Perry was first to exit the championships when he lost on points to the Italian southpaw, Gino Ravaglia. Paddy Lyons was next to bow out when was beaten by the 33-year-old veteran Julius Torma of Czechoslovakia. Torma, who had won gold in the welterweight division at the 1948 London Olympic Games, proved that he still possessed a punch as he shook Lyons with a procession of uppercuts to claim an unanimous verdict – he would go on to claim a bronze in the division in Berlin.

Freddie Gilroy entered the ring the following morning to box the squat and powerful Romanian, Mircea Dobrescu. From Bucharest, Dobrescu had represented his country in the Helsinki Olympic Games and, in 1956, would beat John Caldwell on the way to claiming a silver medal in Melbourne. His pedigree was evident and his strength showed as he dealt easily with everything Freddie could throw at him. In the first round, a wild swing from the Romanian, as he was coming off the ropes, caught Freddie flush on the jaw and sent him to the canvas for a count of eight. It was now a case of damage limitation for the Belfast boy as he climbed gingerly to his feet to back-pedal in the face of an unrelenting attack. The bell saved Gilroy, but it was now only a matter of time. That time duly arrived in the first minute of the second round when the Romanian nailed Freddie with a venomous right hand. Visibly shaken, Gilroy stared into the eyes of the Italian referee, who hesitated briefly before giving the order to box on. Within seconds, Gilroy was sent crumpling to the floor for the third and final time. His dream was over.

Steve Coffey was next to bow out when he lost out convincingly to Finland's Pentti Rautiainen, while Ando Reddy was on the wrong end of a poor decision in his bout with Belgium's Daniel Hellebuyal. To add to Ireland's woes, Paddy Burke lost to the German Rolf Caroli and Eamonn Duffy was well beaten by the Pole, Zdzisław Soczewiński. Ireland never even got near to the medal positions. By the quarterfinals, the team was packing its bags and preparing for the flight home. For the IABA, it had been a chastening exercise that had hit its coffers hard and left the association with nothing to show for it.

CALDWELL IMPRESSES TO TAKE TITLE – NATIONAL SENIOR FINALS 1956

Ulster's boxers took four titles at the National Stadium on St Patrick's night when John Caldwell, Freddie Gilroy, Martin Smith and RUC officer Victor Winnington all boxed superbly. Smith, from the Star club, put in a fantastic display in defeating Gilbert Neill and staking a claim for the featherweight spot on the Irish Olympic team for Melbourne. The surprise of the night was the great showing of Terry Milligan in the middleweight final against the reigning champion, Peter Burke. Milligan, as underdog, showed all his old fire and aggression only to lose the fight on the narrowest of decisions. The best bout of the evening saw a fine display of counter punching by Fred Tiedt, but that was not enough to see off an aggressive display by Harry Perry, whose performance was described in the *Irish Independent* as 'delightful'.

FLYWEIGHT				
(Immaculata)	John Caldwell	*beat*	Private Christy Kelly	(Limerick)
BANTAMWEIGHT				
(St John Bosco)	Freddie Gilroy	*beat*	Corporal Harry Naughton	(Limerick)
FEATHERWEIGHT				
(Star)	Martin Smith	*beat*	Gilbert Neill	(White City)
LIGHTWEIGHT				
(Tredagh)	Tony Byrne	*beat*	Steve Coffey	(Arbour Hill)
LIGHT-WELTERWEIGHT				
(British Railways)	John Sweeney	*walkover*		
WELTERWEIGHT				
(British Railways)	Harry Perry	*beat*	Fred Teidt	(South City)
LIGHT-MIDDLEWEIGHT				
(Crumlin)	Eamonn McKeon	*beat*	Seán McKenna	(St Canice's)
MIDDLEWEIGHT				
(Arbour Hill)	Peter Burke	*beat*	Terry Milligan	(Short and Harland)
LIGHT-HEAVYWEIGHT				
(RUC)	Victor Winnington	*beat*	Mick Gormley	(Crumlin)
HEAVYWEIGHT				
(South City)	Jim Robinson	*beat*	Mick Quinn	(Phoenix)

IRISH GOLDEN GLOVES TOUR – MAY 1956

The Irish team that embarked on the Golden Gloves tour of the US and Canada contained four representatives from Ulster. Alongside John Caldwell and Freddie Gilroy, Belfast's Martin Smith was chosen at featherweight, while, at light-heavyweight, was 25-year-old Victor Winnington. In March 1956, Winnington beat Mick Gormley to become the last-ever RUC man to claim an Irish title. The remaining members of the team were lightweight Tony 'Socks' Byrne, John Sweeney at light-welterweight, Harry Perry at welterweight, Eamonn McKeon at light-middleweight, while Peter Burke at middleweight added extra power to the team. The last boxer to be picked was Jim Robinson at heavyweight, a knock-out specialist who had also travelled to Chicago with the Irish team in 1955.

On 11 May, the team met the Chicago Golden Gloves at the Chicago Stadium where 11,862 spectators had gathered. John Caldwell made an impressive start, outpointing the local champion Pete Melendez. Freddie Gilroy then put Ireland two bouts to the good when he proved too good for Don Eddington, dropping him to the canvas with a sweet left hook in the third round. Martin Smith, however, looked to be in trouble in the first round of his featherweight clash when Detroit's Harry Campbell floored him. The Belfast fighter managed to turn the tables on his opponent and, by the third round, he was, according to the *Chicago Tribune*, 'belting Campbell from one end of the ring to another'. Smith's win was followed by another emphatic performance for Tony Byrne, who beat Ken Eaton on points.

Winning, amazingly, by four bouts to nil, the Irish team thereafter failed to live up to its excellent start. The sting in the tail began with John Sweeney being stopped by Joe Shaw in the third round of their light-welterweight bout. Harry Perry restored Ireland's four-fight cushion with an assured win over Virel Marcey, but it was downhill thereafter for Ireland as Eamonn McKeon and Peter Burke lost their bouts. In front of a fever pitch home crowd, the Americans claimed an unlikely 5-5 draw when Victor Winnington and Jim Robinson were stopped by Ernie Terrell and Solomon McTier respectively. On 16 May, the Irish team travelled to Canada to face a local side and pounded its way to an impressive 7-1 victory with Caldwell knocking Jean Claude Leclair to the canvas on four occasions, while Gilroy and Smith also impressed against their opponents. Surprisingly Harry Perry was beaten in his bout with Eddie Stock. To round off what had been a fantastic tour for the Irish team – and John Caldwell in particular – the Belfast boxer was awarded the Bunny Sabbath Trophy for being the most impressive boxer on display.

BILLY 'SPIDER' KELLY 1932–2010

Billy 'Spider' Kelly's interest in boxing was inevitable, given that his father Jimmy had won both the British and Empire Featherweight titles. Billy was born in Derry in 1932 and fought eighty-four times, winning fifty-six (fifteen by knockout), recording twenty-four defeats and four draws. The undoubted highlight of his career came in 1955, when he emulated his father's achievements by winning the British and Empire Featherweight titles. Kelly built up a large and vociferous following from Derry who travelled in large numbers to see his numerous outings in Belfast's King's Hall. Crowds would form at the arena by mid-afternoon and the rush for the best seats in the balcony was frantic. By the time Kelly would appear in the ring, it was a sure bet that a fair amount of alcohol had been consumed by the patrons.

On Saturday 4 February 1956, Kelly defended his British title over fifteen rounds against Glasgow's Charlie Hill at the south Belfast venue. With a crowd of 10,000 in attendance, Kelly, it seemed, had boxed his way to a convincing win. However, when referee Tommy Little lifted Hill's hand in triumph, a stunned silence fell over the crowd. Initially, all was calm, but then the chants and boos rose to a crescendo. Eventually, beer bottles exploded with froth as they bounced into the ring, followed by the first of a barrage of wooden chairs. The great and the good – including the Lord Mayor of Belfast, Mr Robert Harcourt JP – were hit by flying missiles as the rioting intensified. The Master of Ceremonies, James Allen, was felled in the ring when a chair hit him full on as he attempted to restore calm by leading a rendition of 'When Irish Eyes Are Smiling'. Order was eventually restored only after a series of baton charges within the Hall by the Royal Ulster Constabulary.

That outburst of hooliganism had not been the first time that a Billy Kelly defeat had caused uproar. At the Donnybrook bus depot in Dublin on 27 May 1955, Kelly lost on a close decision for the European title. His opponent, the classy Ray Famechon, had been beaten previously by Willie Pep for the world title, but had agreed to come to Dublin to defend his European crown. When Dutch referee Barend Bergstroem raised Famechon's hand, things turned decidedly nasty. Reporters, seconds, trainers and boxers all took cover in the ring as missiles rained down. Promoter Jack Solomons had a bucket of water thrown over him, while the referee received a punch in the face for his efforts. The Kelly supporters were seething with anger, and the Gardaí were called to restore order. Kelly's career went into decline after his defeat to Hill and his last fight was in the King's Hall in 1962. He died a hero in his native Derry, on 7 May 2010.

GILROY GETS LATE CALL-UP FOR MELBOURNE

Boxing in Banbridge has a long and fine pedigree. However, not a lot of people know that the people of that County Down town were responsible for reigniting the career of one of Ireland's greatest boxers. In September 1956, Belfast's Freddie Gilroy received a devastating blow when he was omitted from the Irish Olympic team bound for Melbourne. Lack of finance was the reason cited by the IABA. However, Gilroy had been Ireland's top amateur over the previous two years and his omission was seen as a slight to the boxer, the St John Bosco club and the Ulster Council. All requests to the IABA to reconsider its position were met with indifference.

There was, however, one avenue left open for Gilroy in his quest for a place on the Melbourne team; that was to raise the £600 needed himself. In 1950s Ireland that amount of money was very hard to come by. It was then that the people of Banbridge enter the story. On Tuesday 30 October 1956, a packed Iveagh Cinema in the town hosted an Ireland *v*. Germany international. The Irish team that night was littered with stars including Gilroy, John Caldwell, Jim Jordan, Martin Smith and Terry Milligan. It was, however, Gilroy who stole the show with a superb victory over the German Albert Nieswano. Such was the ovation for Gilroy that the chairman of the Ulster Council, Captain T.D. Morrison, entered the ring and appealed for the crowd to begin a collection to send Gilroy to Melbourne. Buckets were passed around the audience and a fantastic total of £168 was lifted.

That gesture by the people of Banbridge kick-started the fun and donations soon followed from clubs and county boards throughout Ulster, making the total £361 by 8 November. The Olympic Council of Ireland duly met and gave the Belfast boxer a further week to make up the difference. With the 600 workers in Gilroy's Beltex factory all subscribing to the fund, the shortfall was met and, with only two days left for nominations, the Irish Olympic Council endorsed Gilroy's name as Ireland's bantamweight representative.

IRELAND'S BOXING GLORY – MELBOURNE 1956

The Irish boxing team that travelled to Melbourne in 1956 and claimed three bronze and a silver medal, was hindered by a lack of finances. As well as Freddie Gilroy, Tony 'Socks' Byrne also had to rely on the generosity of the people of Drogheda, who raised over £630 to send the Tredagh man to the Games. In the heavyweight division, Ireland selected Donegal's Pat Sharkey, a former Irish junior and Scottish champion, who was working in Queensland at the time, thus saving on expenses. In an act of extreme parsimony, Sharkey, who was defeated in his opening contest, was asked by Irish officials to leave the Olympic Village.

Freddie Gilroy caused a sensation in his first outing against the double European finalist, Russia's Boris Stepanov, by knocking him out in the third round of their contest. He battled his way to the semi-finals only to be eliminated on a casting vote of the Russian referee against the German, Wolfgang Behrendt. John Caldwell in the opening round of the flyweight division was afforded a bye. His first opponent, Yai Shwe of Burma, fell victim to John's unique style of working inside with quick punches and then switching his attacks from body to head. Yai Shwe was duly knocked out in the third round. In the quarterfinal, Caldwell silenced the legions of Melbourne fans when he beat their local hero, Warren Batchelor. The Australian had been the favourite to win the gold medal but Caldwell's success put him in pole position for the gold medal. However, it was not to be as in the semi-final Caldwell lost out to the crack Romanian Mircea Dobrescu and had to content himself with a bronze medal.

Tony Byrne's first fight in Melbourne saw the Drogheda man drawn to meet the Czech, Josef Chovanec. Byrne was victorious in that bout when his opponent was disqualified in the third round. Standing just three rounds away from a bronze medal, Byrne was drawn against the American champion, Louis Molina. A tough battle ensued which Byrne won on a points decision. Byrne's opponent in the semi-final was to be the West German Harry Kurschat. In an international earlier that year, Byrne had defeated the German who had beaten Kurschat in their national championships and expectations were high. It was not to be, however, as the German displayed greater technique and scoring ability to get the decision over Byrne on points.

Fred Tiedt had fought his way to the semi-finals where he met the Australian Kevin Hogarth in front of a partisan home crowd. The South City boxer put in an exemplary display as he kept out of the Australian's reach for the duration of the fight. Waiting in the final was the fancied Romanian, Nicolas Linca. Tiedt seemed to have done everything right throughout the fight but his controversial loss to Linca was widely derided. The renowned boxing author and editor of *The Ring* magazine, Nat Fleischer, described the result as 'the most disgraceful decision I have ever witnessed'. The anomaly was that Tiedt had been awarded more points in total than the Romanian, but was denied on the majority verdict.

It was said that Lord Killanin (President of the Irish Olympic Council) had been asked by an official at the end of the bout to make his way to the ring for the presentation in the belief that the result had gone in Tiedt's favour. Wisely, Killanin retained his seat, not wishing to tempt fate. A Romanian referee was heard saying to Lord Killanan that Linca had been well beaten. However, it was Tiedt who took the verdict squarely on the chin. Interestingly, in the Official Report on the 1956 Games, as produced by the International Olympic Committee, the fight between Tiedt and Linca was mentioned specifically in dispatches: 'Welterweight: Probably the most unlucky boxer was Tiedt (Ireland) who lost a close final to Linca (Romania) after he had come through three very hard fights in his division against Aaleskra (Poland), Lane (USA) and Hogarth (Australia).'

Fred was later to recall that, after the fight, he had tried to lodge an official complaint, but was told by officials that he was required to lodge £5 for it to be heard. Of course, neither he nor any of the Irish officials had £5 to spare and the result stood.

Flyweight	John Caldwell
Bantamweight	Freddie Gilroy
Featherweight	Martin Smyth
Lightweight	Tony Byrne
Light-welterweight	Harry Perry
Welterweight	Fred Tiedt
and Heavyweight	Pat Sharkey

'SOCKS' BEATS OLYMPIC CHAMPION – IRELAND *v.* ENGLAND 1957

The winner of the lightweight title at the Melbourne Games was the stylish Scot Dick McTaggart, who was deemed untouchable in the amateur game at the time. Tony Byrne had watched McTaggart win the gold in Melbourne and was frustrated in knowing that he could have been in the ring with 'Dandy Dick' that evening. Byrne was afforded an opportunity to meet the golden boy of British boxing at the Royal Albert Hall on 30 January 1957. McTaggart, who was representing England as a member of the Royal Air Force, was fancied to win the bout easily. The Drogheda man, though, fought the fight of his life with a ferocity seldom seen in an amateur bout to claim victory over the champion. He caught McTaggart in the second round to send him to the canvas and was awarded the bout after three bruising rounds. Despite the scarcity of televisions, the fight was witnessed live by thousands of people on Drogheda who packed pubs and houses to see the local hero claim his win.

EIGHT TITLES FOR DUBLIN – NATIONAL SENIOR FINALS 1957

It was predicted to be the fight of the century and it lived up to its name, as Harry Perry lost his welterweight title to Fred Teidt. As holder of titles at various weights since 1952, Perry was, however, second best to Tiedt on the night. In a rematch of the 1956 final, Tiedt reversed the decision, fighting like a panther in a bout that left the packed arena gasping for its breath. A feature of the night saw brothers Peter and Ollie Byrne claim titles at light-middleweight and light-heavyweight respectively. John Caldwell retained his flyweight title with a most impressive performance against Peter Lavery. On the night, eight titles went to Dublin clubs. The other two went to Belfast. Freddie Gilroy had turned professional in January that year.

	FLYWEIGHT			
(De La Salle)	John Caldwell	*beat*	Peter Lavery	(St John Bosco)
	BANTAMWEIGHT			
(Avona)	Paddy Courtney	*beat*	Packie Leahy	(Tipperary)
	FEATHERWEIGHT			
(Sandymount)	Tommy Reddy	*beat*	Tommy Maxwell	(St John Bosco)
	LIGHTWEIGHT			
(St George's)	Jim Jordan	*beat*	Des Leahy	(Ranelagh)
	LIGHT-WELTERWEIGHT			
(Crumlin)	Mick Reid	*beat*	Johnny Martin	(Cork)
	WELTERWEIGHT			
(South City)	Fred Tiedt	*beat*	Harry Perry	(British Railways)
	LIGHT-MIDDLEWEIGHT			
(Avona)	Peter Byrne	*beat*	Danny McEntee	(Monaghan)
	MIDDLEWEIGHT			
(Crumlin)	Eamonn McKeon	*beat*	Colm McCoy	(Kilcullen)
	LIGHT-HEAVYWEIGHT			
(St Andrew's)	Ollie Byrne	*beat*	Terry Milligan	(Short and Harland)
	HEAVYWEIGHT			
(Arbour Hill)	Paddy Lyons	*beat*	Mick Quinn	(Phoenix)

PERRY SHADES TIEDT IN YET ANOTHER CLASSIC: NATIONAL SENIOR FINALS 1958

The final of the welterweight division on 22 March again brought Fred Tiedt and Harry Perry together. It was a bout fought at a frantic speed with accurate punching and masterful defensive boxing on show throughout. The Perry supporters erupted when he was adjudged to have been the winner, but to many observers the fight had been too close to call. Tiedt had Perry on the ropes on a number of occasions, but his lack of a telling punch was evident throughout. The Tiedt versus Perry fight overshadowed the rest of the bill. It was a rivalry that would enter the annals of Irish boxing as, without doubt, the greatest series of bouts ever witnessed in the National Stadium. At flyweight, Belfast's Peter Lavery was victorious in seeing off Christy Kelly. Dublin clubs claimed eight of the ten titles, with the other two going to Belfast.

	FLYWEIGHT			
(St John Bosco)	Peter Lavery	*beat*	Christy Kelly	(Limerick)
	BANTAMWEIGHT			
(Avona)	Paddy Courtney	*beat*	Charlie Dunne	(Ranelagh)
	FEATHERWEIGHT			
(Holy Family)	John McClory	*beat*	Jimmy Martin	(Mount Street)
	LIGHTWEIGHT			
(Corinthians)	Tommy Butler	*beat*	Christy Kelly	(Sandymount)
	LIGHT-WELTERWEIGHT			
(Avona)	George Arnold	*beat*	Brian Spain	(Sandymount)
	WELTERWEIGHT			
(British Railways)	Harry Perry	*beat*	Fred Tiedt	(St Andrew's)
	LIGHT-MIDDLEWEIGHT			
(British Railways)	Ando Power	*beat*	Gerry Henry	(Dundalk)
	MIDDLEWEIGHT			
(Crumlin)	Eamonn McKeon	*beat*	Colm McCoy	(Kilcullen)
	LIGHT-HEAVYWEIGHT			
(St Andrew's)	Ollie Byrne	*beat*	Jim Carroll	(Wicklow)
	HEAVYWEIGHT			
(St Andrew's)	Paddy Lyons	*beat*	Jim Robinson	(St Andrew's)

MILLIGAN MISTAKES THE PRINCE FOR THE POPE

In 1958, at the Cardiff Empire Games, none other than Prince Philip, the grand old Duke of Edinburgh, presented Belfast and Ireland amateur legend Terry Milligan with his gold medal after the middleweight final. The eminent prince, patron of the Games, congratulated the Irishman on his achievement and, in his well-clipped upper-class tones, said, 'Well done, my man, you fought an absolutely superb fight out there.' Terry, a humble man, was somewhat star-struck to be facing one of the most famous men in the world. His response was epic, as he replied to the prince, 'Why, thank you very much, your, ah, em, Holiness?' That story probably gets a run out at Buckingham Palace every Christmas!

NINE NEW CHAMPIONS CROWNED – NATIONAL SENIOR FINALS 1959

Ollie Byrne was the only boxer to retain his title on a night that saw nine new champions crowned at the National Stadium. His victory over Maurice Loughran was shrouded in controversy as the Monaghan man went to the canvas claiming to have been hit low. The referee counted Loughran out regardless. At flyweight, Adam McClean of the Crown club in Belfast gave a superb display to outpoint Christy Kelly of Limerick, who was floored three times in the opening round. Seán Brown, sparring partner of future British bantamweight champion Freddie Gilroy, took the honours against Sandymount's Eddie Kelly. Harry Perry was unable to defend his title due to a damaged thumb. The featherweight crown was won by Liam Ralph, who beat the hot favourite David Buckley on a cut-eye stoppage. Buckley was an intriguing boxer who, despite having a physically 'under-developed' right arm, had beaten both Ando and Tommy Reddy on his way to the final. A year later, boxing officials prevented Buckley from competing due to his arm. In 2000, he was inducted into the IABA's Hall of Fame.

	FLYWEIGHT			
(Crown)	Adam McClean	*beat*	Christy Kelly	(Limerick)
	BANTAMWEIGHT			
(Ranelagh)	Charlie Dunne	*beat*	Des Andrews	(St Andrew's)
	FEATHERWEIGHT			
(Thurles)	Liam Ralph	*beat*	David Buckley	(Mallow)
	LIGHTWEIGHT			
(British Railways)	Mick Harvey	*beat*	Tommy Murphy	(Drogheda)
	LIGHT-WELTERWEIGHT			
(St John Bosco)	Seán Brown	*beat*	Eddie Kelly	(Sandymount)
	WELTERWEIGHT			
(Crumlin)	Mick Reid	*beat*	Jimmy McLoughlin	(Sandymount)
	LIGHT-MIDDLEWEIGHT			
(Arbour Hill)	Willie Byrne	*beat*	Jim Larkin	(North City)
	MIDDLEWEIGHT			
(Kilcullen)	Colm McCoy	*beat*	Eamonn McKeon	(Crumlin)
	LIGHT-HEAVYWEIGHT			
(St Andrew's)	Ollie Byrne	*beat*	Maurice Loughran	(Monaghan)
	HEAVYWEIGHT			
(Guinness)	Mick Gormley	*beat*	Paddy Lyons	(Arbour Hill)

THREE BRONZE MEDALS FOR IRELAND – LUCERNE 1959

In 1959, Harry Perry represented Ireland at his third major games at the European Boxing Championships in Lucerne, Switzerland, and won a bronze medal. That year, Perry had not fought for the Irish title due to damage he had received to the thumb of his right hand. By the time the team had been selected, he had recovered sufficiently to secure the welterweight nomination. Perry was fancied to go far in the championships due to his wealth of experience. However, once again, Lady Luck was to desert him. In his first bout, the Dubliner was lucky to record a victory over the Bulgarian, Schischman Mizew.

That fight was too close to call but may have swung Perry's way due to a warning Mizew received in the first round for hitting after being told to break. Three right hooks to Perry's jaw in the last round left the decision too tight to call. Harry was considered fortunate to win. His next contest was to see him an easy winner over the Dane Benn Neilsen. However, during the last round, a ligament snapped in his lower leg. The last minute was fought out in agony by Perry. He won convincingly to assure himself at least a bronze medal, but the prospect of a semi-final outing was doubtful. He recalled, 'The injury was serious as I would be hindered badly in the final, however it turned out. They tried everything, strapped it up, and put ice on it, but the tournament doctors took one look at it and said that I would be unable to fight in the semi-final.' Perry, along with Adam McClean and Colm McCoy, claimed bronze medals for Ireland at the Lucerne championships.

6

THE 1960s

PAINFUL TEARS FOR SEÁN BROWN – NATIONAL SENIOR FINALS 1960

Defending light-welterweight champion Seán Brown found Bernie Meli too hot to handle in the 1960 light-welterweight decider and burst helplessly into pitiful tears as referee Charlie Evenden stopped their fight in the second round. The best fight on the night saw Colm McCoy take the light-heavyweight title from the reigning champion, Ollie Byrne. In a fight described as a 'ding-dong struggle', the last three minutes had the crowd on its feet, roaring for both boxers. It was McCoy's accuracy and power that swung the decision in his favour. In the middleweight decider, Dublin inter-county hurler Jim Byrne took the title with a split decision over Eamonn McKeon and duly left the Stadium to travel to Cork for a national league game the following day. The bill was a spectacular success with the packed house being entertained by 'endless enjoyment and thrill a minute contests', according to the *Irish Press*.

		FLYWEIGHT		
(Crown)	Adam McClean	*beat*	Wilf Megarry	(Glenburn)
		BANTAMWEIGHT		
(Coventry)	Paddy Kenny	*beat*	John Joe Donaghy	(Coalisland)
		FEATHERWEIGHT		
(Sandymount)	Ando Reddy	*beat*	Tommy McEvoy	(Birmingham)
		LIGHTWEIGHT		
(11th Hussars)	Corporal Danny O'Brien	*beat*	Tommy Murphy	(Drogheda)
		LIGHT-WELTERWEIGHT		
(Immaculata)	Bernie Meli	*beat*	Seán Brown	(St John Bosco)
		WELTERWEIGHT		
(British Railways)	Harry Perry	*beat*	Seamus Gallagher	(Ballyshannon)
		LIGHT-MIDDLEWEIGHT		
(British Railways)	Ando Power	*beat*	Mick Reid	(Garda)

	MIDDLEWEIGHT			
(Arbour Hill)	Jim Byrne	*beat*	Eamonn McKeon	(Crumlin)

	LIGHT-HEAVYWEIGHT			
(Kilcullen)	Colm McCoy	*beat*	Ollie Byrne	(St Andrew's)

	HEAVYWEIGHT			
(Garda)	Joe Casey	*beat*	Paddy Lyons	(Arbour Hill)

BOXERS OUT OF LUCK –
ROME OLYMPIC GAMES 1960

Still basking in the glory of the achievements of the Irish boxers in Melbourne in 1956, Ireland sent a ten-man boxing team to Rome in 1960. However, it was to be a disappointing and expensive trip as one by one the boxers exited the competition. Five of the boxers, Paddy Kenny, Ando Reddy, Danny O'Brien, Bernie Meli and Eamonn McKeon, all won bouts at the Games, but the lack of medals was an acute setback for the Irish boxing on the international stage. It became evident that Ireland's boxing style and technique was lacking as the sport was changing utterly in tactical terms. This had become evident as Eastern European countries set a fantastic pace throughout the tournament. There was particular disappointment for Ireland's three medallists at the 1959 European Championships, Harry Perry, Adam McClean and Colm McCoy.

The most contentious decision saw Cork's Pat Kenny lose on a split decision to the USA's Jerry Armstrong. Two of the five judges had voted for Kenny, while two had opted for Armstrong, who had fought on the defensive throughout the contest. The fifth judge, who had scored the bout evenly, inexplicably gave the American the decision with his casting vote. Irish officials lodged a protest, but to no avail. Such was the criticism of the overall standard of adjudication that the Olympic Committee sacked over half the judges at the quarterfinals stage. Notably, after his win over Greece's Dimitrios Mikhail, Belfast's Bernie Meli was afforded a standing ovation by guests of honour Prince Rainier and Princess Grace Kelly. However, Meli was to exit the competition in his following bout when he lost to the Czech, Bohumil Němeček, the eventual gold medallist in the light-welterweight division.

Flyweight	Adam McClean
Bantamweight	Paddy Kenny
Featherweight	Ando Reddy
Lightweight	Danny O'Brien
Light-welterweight	Bernie Meli

Welterweight	Harry Perry
Light-middleweight	Mick Reid
Middleweight	Eamonn McKeon
Light-heavyweight	Colm McCoy
Heavyweight	Joe Casey

OLLIE TAKES HIS FOURTH TITLE – NATIONAL SENIOR FINALS 1961

It was standing room only at the National Stadium on St Patrick's evening in 1961 when only four champions retained titles. Ollie Byrne had the crowd on its feet as he took his fourth title with a hard-fought win over favourite Colm McCoy. In the flyweight class, Wilf Megarry reversed his defeat in 1960 to fellow Belfast boxer Adam McClean. A clean right cross to McClean's jaw sent the champion to the canvas in the second round and ended the contest in Megarry's favour. In the bantamweight decider, 18-year-old Dubliner Eddie Tracey claimed his first title when he beat the reigning champion Paddy Kenny on points. Drogheda's Tommy Murphy, future president of the IABA, took his first senior crown by seeing off Willie Rea in the lightweight division, showing some tremendous defensive skill in the process. The middleweight bout between brothers Willie and Jim Byrne was conceded sportingly by reigning champion Jim.

	FLYWEIGHT			
(Glenburn)	Wilf Megarry	beat	Adam McClean	(Crown)
	BANTAMWEIGHT			
(Avona)	Eddie Treacy	beat	Paddy Kenny	(Coventry)
	LIGHTWEIGHT			
(Drogheda)	Tommy Murphy	beat	Willie Rea	(St Malachy's)
	FEATHERWEIGHT			
(Sandymount)	Ando Reddy	beat	Charlie Dunne	(Ranelagh)
	LIGHT-WELTERWEIGHT			
(Immaculata)	Bernie Meli	beat	Jim Magowan	(Achilles)
	WELTERWEIGHT			
(British Railways)	Harry Perry	beat	Bob Sempey	(Star)
	LIGHT-MIDDLEWEIGHT			
(British Railways)	Ando Power	beat	Teddy Joyce	(Arbour Hill)
	MIDDLEWEIGHT			
(Arbour Hill)	Willie Byrne	*walkover*		
	LIGHT-HEAVYWEIGHT			
(Guinness)	Ollie Byrne	beat	Colm McCoy	(Kilcullen)
	HEAVYWEIGHT			
(Arbour Hill)	Joe Casey	beat	Tommy Bruce	(Sandymount)

IRISH AMATEUR BOXING ASSOCIATION – JUBILEE TOURNAMENT 1961

In celebration of its fiftieth anniversary, the Irish Amateur Boxing Association hosted a home nations' jubilee tournament in the National Stadium in December 1961. After the preliminary rounds, Irish boxers claimed seven places in the finals on Friday 8 December. The host nation had to be content with only two titles coming courtesy of Wilf Megarry at flyweight, and Harry Perry at welterweight. Both Wales and Scotland claimed three wins each, while England, which had been tipped to take a clean sweep of titles, had to be content with two.

Megarry reversed a previous defeat to England's Alan Rudkin on a majority verdict in the flyweight decider. Rudkin would, as a professional, would win both British and European crowns and lose twice for the undisputed world bantamweight title. However, Perry's win was marred as his opponent Johnny Prichett picked up a cut in the third round and was forced to retire. Pritchett would go on to win a Lonsdale Belt in 1966 as British middleweight champion. In his final bout as an amateur, England's power-puncher Billy Walker took less than a round to stop Jim Monaghan in the heavyweight final. Ireland's other finalists were Eddie Tracey, Pat McGrane, Alan Galbraith and Willie Byrne.

REDDY BOWS OUT, PERRY MARCHES ON – NATIONAL SENIOR FINALS 1962

The 1962 senior finals saw Ando Reddy retire from amateur boxing as his attempt to gain a seventh title was thwarted by Kilcullen's Willie Schwer. Having won his first title in 1951, Reddy lost on a split decision and received a standing ovation in the National Stadium as he announced his retirement after the featherweight final. Walter Henry from the St George's club exploded on to the boxing scene when he dispatched defending champion Wilf Megarry in one round to take the flyweight title. A cut eye suffered by Megarry officially caused the stoppage, but Henry's superiority was such that he was well on his way to knocking his opponent out. Wilf Megarry was to die tragically in a car crash in Zambia in 1966 at the age of 26. The son of a Belfast publican, Megarry had been working in Africa as an engineer.

Harry Perry, fresh from winning the British Railways title in London the previous evening, took his record ninth title when he overwhelmed Gabriel Young of the Achilles club with a superb performance that was described as 'perpetual motion' by the *Irish Independent*. Harry Perry announced his retirement soon after. He boxed British champion and fellow Melbourne Olympian Freddie Gilroy in a farewell exhibition bout at the National Stadium on 8 February 1963.

		FLYWEIGHT		
(Belfast)	Walter Henry	*beat*	Wilf Megarry	(Belfast)
		BANTAMWEIGHT		
(Terenure)	Joe Coyne	*beat*	Jim Houlihan	(Avona)
		LIGHTWEIGHT		
(Drogheda)	Tommy Murphy	*beat*	Tommy Campbell	(Star, Belfast)
		FEATHERWEIGHT		
(Kilcullen)	Willie Schwer	*beat*	Ando Reddy	(Sandymount)
		LIGHT-WELTERWEIGHT		
(Immaculata)	Bernie Meli	*beat*	John Maloney	(Sandymount)
		WELTERWEIGHT		
(British Railways)	Harry Perry	*beat*	Gabriel Young	(Achilles)
		LIGHT-MIDDLEWEIGHT		
(British Railways)	Ando Power	*beat*	Mick Reid	(Garda)
		MIDDLEWEIGHT		
(Arbour Hill)	Willie Byrne	*beat*	Barney Wilson	(Immaculata)
		LIGHT-HEAVYWEIGHT		
(Belfast)	Ivan Christie	*walkover*		
		HEAVYWEIGHT		
(Cork)	Donal Murray	*beat*	Jim Monaghan	(Derry)

FREDDIE GILROY *v.* JOHN CALDWELL – OCTOBER 1962

After winning bronze medals for Ireland at the 1956 Olympic Games, both Freddie Gilroy and John Caldwell soon fought their way to world dominance in the professional bantamweight and flyweight divisions respectively. In October 1960, Gilroy was to lose on a disputed decision to Alphonse Halimi for the European version of the world bantamweight title. Despite being promised a rematch, Gilroy was left reeling when promoter Jack Solomons offered Caldwell the chance to meet Halimi for the title in May 1961. In what was his first outing as a bantamweight, Caldwell took the title in fine style at the Wembley Arena and secured a crack at Eder Jofre for the undisputed world title in Brazil in January 1962. Caldwell was well beaten that night and soon a clash with Gilroy was secured for an eagerly anticipated battle at the King's Hall in October 1962. In typical Belfast style, the meeting of these two greats caught the imagination of the city and their clash on 20 October 1962 drew a record-breaking 16,000 spectators. In the midst of the Cuban Missile Crisis, Belfast's two superpowers met in a highly charged arena. At stake were the British and Empire bantamweight titles and the fight was an all-action encounter which had the crowd on their feet. By the ninth round, John Caldwell's eye had been cut badly and he was forced to retire. The boxing public cried out for a rematch, but Gilroy retired from the ring in the aftermath of the fight and it was never to be.

ARBOUR HILL'S GLORY NIGHT – NATIONAL SENIOR FINALS 1963

Ulster's representatives had been expected to lift eight of the senior titles on Friday 22 March, but had to be content with only four on a night of upsets at the stadium. The main surprise saw Des Leahy outpoint Charlie Rice over three gruelling rounds in the welterweight final. Doagh's Henry Turkington was out-boxed by Teddy Joyce in another shock on the night and future Olympic bronze medallist 18-year-old Jim McCourt claimed his first title when he was a clear winner over the 1962 champion, Willie Schwer. Arbour Hill took four titles, the most impressive of which was Joyce's win over Turkington.

	FLYWEIGHT			
(St John Bosco)	Seán McCafferty	*beat*	Corporal Tommy Connolly	(St Barbara's)
	BANTAMWEIGHT			
(Hollerith)	Jimmy Henry	*beat*	Jackie Gaffney	(Corinthians)
	FEATHERWEIGHT			
(Immaculata)	Jim McCourt	*beat*	Willie Schwer	(Luton)
	LIGHTWEIGHT			
(Arbour Hill)	Liam Clarke	*beat*	Eddie Tracey	(Arbour Hill)
	LIGHT-WELTERWEIGHT			
(White City)	Jim Neill	*beat*	Tommy Armour	(Lisburn)
	WELTERWEIGHT			
(Terenure)	Des Leahy	*beat*	Charlie Rice	(Holy Family)
	LIGHT-MIDDLEWEIGHT			
(Arbour Hill)	Teddy Joyce	*beat*	Henry Turkington	(Doagh)
	MIDDLEWEIGHT			
(Guinness)	Jack O'Rourke	*beat*	Eamon Smith	(Phoenix)
	LIGHT-HEAVYWEIGHT			
(Arbour Hill)	Willie Byrne	*beat*	Mick Harris	(Derry)
	HEAVYWEIGHT			
(Arbour Hill)	Jim Byrne	*beat*	Joe Casey	(Arbour Hill)

SONNY LISTON VISITS IRELAND

Fresh from knocking out Floyd Patterson for the second time, Sonny Liston toured Europe in 1963. After visiting Sweden, he boxed exhibitions in Scotland and Ireland, including a visit to the Ulster Hall in Belfast.

The world champion arrived at the Belfast venue for an exhibition but the audience felt somewhat short-changed by what they saw. The world champion skipped along to his theme song 'Night Train', sparred two opponents and then left the arena. The patrons were less than impressed!

Earlier that day, Margaret Jameson, a 21-year-old Belfast store model, lost her job for taking time off work to kiss the champion Liston at a party in a rival shop. Margaret joined thousands trying to catch a glimpse and was asked by a photographer to plant a kiss on the champion's cheek. 'I wondered what he looked like,' Margaret explained. 'He looks so tough in his photographs, so I went along with the photographer's suggestion,' she added. When her boss, George Major, saw his employee's picture in the *Belfast Telegraph*, he sacked her, declaring, 'If all our staff visited rival stores during working hours, where would we be?' Margaret said she thought the decision was unfair. However, Liston left Belfast unaware of all the fuss.

TOKYO PLACES CLAIMED – NATIONAL SENIOR FINALS 1964

With the Olympic Games taking place in Tokyo in October that year, the 1964 finals took on greater importance for the competitors. In the flyweight class, Seán McCafferty put down a marker by outclassing the Luton-based Paddy Maguire. Maguire would go on to claim the Irish title in 1965 and the British ABA crown in 1966, but on the night McCafferty put in a masterful display that booked him his place on the Irish Olympic team. The biggest upset of the night came when Dave Barbour defeated the seasoned international Ivan Christie in the light-heavyweight final. Barbour, who was in his first season as a senior, made no errors throughout the final, catching Christy with barrages of neat and accurate punches. As usual, the principal bouts were broadcast live between nine and ten o'clock that evening on RTÉ Radio, with commentary from Philip Greene and summaries by Harry Perry.

	FLYWEIGHT			
(St John Bosco)	Seán McCafferty	*beat*	Paddy Maguire	(Vauxhall)
	BANTAMWEIGHT			
(Hollerith)	Jimmy Henry	*walkover*		
	FEATHERWEIGHT			
(St Matthews)	Paddy Fitzsimons	*beat*	Rory Byrne	(Transport)
	LIGHTWEIGHT			
(Dominic Savio)	Jim McCourt	*beat*	Paddy McGrane	(British Railways)
	LIGHT-WELTERWEIGHT			
(North Irish Horse)	Jim Neill	*beat*	Paddy Keogh	(British Rail)

	WELTERWEIGHT			
(Crumlin)	Seamus Mahon	*walkover*		

	LIGHT-MIDDLEWEIGHT			
(Crumlin)	Liam Mullen	*beat*	Tom Heneghan	(Castlebar)

	MIDDLEWEIGHT			
(Crown)	Barney Burns	*beat*	John Grace	(Carrick-on-Suir)

	LIGHT-HEAVYWEIGHT			
(Crumlin)	Dave Barbour	*beat*	Ivan Christie	(South Belfast)

	HEAVYWEIGHT			
(British Railways)	Tony Brogan	*beat*	Pat O'Keeffe	(Queen's University)

JIM MCCOURT TAKES BRONZE – TOKYO OLYMPIC GAMES 1964

When Jim McCourt took his place on the rostrum in Tokyo to claim a bronze medal in the lightweight class, he became the sixth Irish boxer to collect Olympic honours. Four of those six boxers had come from Belfast, including three, John McNally, John Caldwell and McCourt, who had begun their careers at the Immaculata club. To reach the semi-final, McCourt had won three bouts on convincing 4-1 score lines. However, his defeat to the Russian Velikton Barannikov on a split decision was considered to have been an injustice. At flyweight, Seán McCafferty, an unnatural southpaw who modelled his style on his hero Freddie Gilroy, won his first two bouts before going out in the quarterfinal to the eventual gold medallist, Fernando Atzori of Italy. Chris Rafter, who lost out to John Caldwell for a place at the 1956 Olympics, had left Ireland for the United States a year later, where he won three Chicago Golden Gloves titles. In 1964, the 27-year-old was based in Asia with the US Army and was chosen as Ireland's bantamweight representative in Tokyo. However, he was defeated in the first round of competition when he lost to the Argentine Abel Almerez. The Irish team was coached by Belfast schoolteacher Harry Enright, who sadly passed away during the writing of this book, aged 84.

Flyweight	Seán McCafferty
Bantamweight	Chris Rafter
Featherweight	Paddy Fitzsimons
Lightweight	Jim McCourt
Light-welterweight	Brian Anderson

OLYMPIC CHAMPION BEATEN IN DUBLIN

The international clash between Ireland and Poland in Dublin on Saturday 6 March 1965, offered Belfast's Jim McCourt the tantalising prospect of a crack at the Olympic champion, Józef Grudzień. In Tokyo, the previous year, McCourt had been on the wrong end of a hotly disputed decision in his semi-final to the Russian Velikton Barannikov, who lost out to Grudzień for the gold medal. In a duel of absorbing intensity, the Olympic champion shaded the first round against McCourt in front of a packed National Stadium. However, in the second round, the Belfast lightweight took command, slipping Grudzień's lead to score heavily to the head and body. In the last round, McCourt landed a sweet left cross to the Pole's jaw, shaking the champion's composure. From then until the final bell McCourt put in a display of assured defensive boxing to shade the fight on a split decision, with only the Polish judge awarding the verdict to Grudzień. McCourt's victory was greeted with unrestrained and prolonged delight by the partisan crowd. Earlier, Willie Turkington had been beaten in the light-welterweight class by Jerzy Kulej, the gold medallist in Tokyo in 1964. However, Ireland was to lose the match 6-4 to a technically gifted side, with McCourt, Ivan Christie, Brian Anderson and Liam Mullen victorious for the home team.

CLARKE SHOCKS MCCOURT – NATIONAL SENIOR FINALS 1965

Just three weeks after his heroics on international duty against Poland, Jim McCourt relinquished his Irish title to Arbour Hill's Liam Clarke. With forty seconds left in the second round, the referee was forced to stop the bout after McCourt sustained a cut eye and the decision then went to the judges. With both boxers tied on points, Clarke was awarded the bout for his greater aggression, to the delight of the crowd. Only two champions succeeded in retaining their titles, with Barney Burns of the Crown club proving too clever for John Grace, while Dave Barbour picked his punches superbly in seeing off Jim Byrne of Arbour Hill. Both Seán McCafferty and Paddy Fitzsimons, champions and Olympians in 1964, had joined the professional ranks with Belfast promoter Barney Eastwood.

	FLYWEIGHT			
(Vauxhall)	Paddy Maguire	*walkover*		
	BANTAMWEIGHT			
(Carrick-on-Suir)	Nick Butler	*beat*	Paddy Reilly	(Corinthians)
	FEATHERWEIGHT			
(Arbour Hill)	Eddie Tracey	*beat*	Terry Tyrell	(St Saviour's)
	LIGHTWEIGHT			
(Arbour Hill)	Liam Clarke	*beat*	Jim McCourt	(Dominic Savio)
	LIGHT-WELTERWEIGHT			
(London)	Brian Anderson	*beat*	John Maloney	(Port of Dublin)

	WELTERWEIGHT			
(St John Bosco)	Willie Turkington	beat	Tommy Murphy	(Drogheda)

	LIGHT-MIDDLEWEIGHT			
(Banbridge)	Eamon McCusker	beat	Liam Mullen	(Crumlin)

	MIDDLEWEIGHT			
(Crown)	Barney Burns	beat	John Grace	(Port of Dublin)

	LIGHT-HEAVYWEIGHT			
(Crumlin)	Dave Barbour	beat	Jim Byrne	(Arbour Hill)

	HEAVYWEIGHT			
(Port of Dublin)	Jack O'Rourke	beat	Eddie Smith	(Avona)

THE NIGHT OF THE TWO PADDY MAGUIRES – NATIONAL SENIOR FINALS 1966

It was a night on which two Paddy Maguires appeared in the finals, with only the Belfast version victorious in the bantamweight class. In a 'punch-up that caught the imagination of the crowd', Kilcullen's Christy Ennis met an 'indestructible tank' in the Belfast Maguire, who took the title with a unanimous points verdict. The middleweight title went to southpaw Seán O'Sullivan, a Belfast-born British soldier who had represented England against Ireland in London in 1966. The only other successful titleholder was the heavyweight Jack O'Rourke, who stopped the tall and thin John McKinty, another Belfast-born British soldier, in the second round of a contest. That bout had been a tame affair until O'Rourke livened the exchanges with some neat and powerful hooks which caught McKinty with precision. Liam Clarke of the Arbour Hill club won Boxer of the Tournament and impressed greatly during his win over Sammy Lockhart.

	FLYWEIGHT			
(Hollerith)	Paddy Graham	beat	Paddy Maguire	(Luton)

	BANTAMWEIGHT			
(South Belfast)	Paddy Maguire	beat	Christy Ennis	(Kilcullen)

	FEATHERWEIGHT			
(St Saviour's)	Terry Tyrrell	walkover		

	LIGHTWEIGHT			
(Arbour Hill)	Liam Clarke	beat	Sammy Lockhart	(Achilles)

	LIGHT-WELTERWEIGHT			
(Immaculata)	Jim McCourt	beat	Seamus Mahon	(Crumlin)

	WELTERWEIGHT			
(Dominic Savio)	Frankie Young	beat	Seán Harty	(Edgewick)

	LIGHT-MIDDLEWEIGHT			
(St John Bosco)	Gus Farrell	beat	Eamon McCusker	(Banbridge)

	MIDDLEWEIGHT			
(De La Salle)	Seán O'Sullivan	beat	Tom McGreevy	(Dublin University)

		LIGHT-HEAVYWEIGHT		
(Crumlin)	John Riordan	*beat*	Kevin Treacy	(De La Salle)

		HEAVYWEIGHT		
(Port of Dublin)	Jack O'Rourke	*beat*	John McKinty	(De La Salle)

TRAGIC DEATH IN A DUBLIN RING

The death of 19-year-old Gerard O'Brien on 23 January 1967, after being knocked out at the Transport Club in Dublin, sent shockwaves through the Irish world of sport. O'Brien had been taking part in a bout in the County Dublin League on 19 January, when he took a right hand to the jaw from his opponent, Joe Farrell, and fell to the canvas, banging his head. It was O'Brien's second bout as an amateur and he was carried from the ring unconscious and transferred to the Richmond Hospital where he died four days later. At the inquest into the death, a finding of accidental death was returned by the coroner, Dr P.J. Boffin. He added that it was important to put on the record that both Gerard's opponent and the referee, Benny Carabini, were 'entirely blameless' for the boxer's death. It was the first recorded death of a boxer in an Irish ring and an emotional Joe Farrell said afterwards that he would never box again.

MCCARTHY SHOCKS LOCKHART – IRISH SENIOR FINALS 1967

A display of clever defensive boxing by Mick McCarthy saw him provide the shock of the night by defeating Sammy Lockhart in the lightweight decider. Jim McCourt retained his title after a tough battle with Lisburn's John Rodgers, while Banbridge's Eamon McCusker was sent to the canvas within thirty seconds of his light-middleweight clash with Willie Cullen. McCusker fought back courageously and in the second round the referee was forced to intervene to prevent Cullen receiving any further punishment.

		FLYWEIGHT		
(Arbour Hill)	Brendan McCarthy	*beat*	Harry Cunningham	(St Matthew's)

		BANTAMWEIGHT		
(Holy Family)	Sammy Vernon	*beat*	Paddy Maguire	(Immaculata)

		FEATHERWEIGHT		
(Immaculata)	Jim McAuley	*beat*	Paddy Graham	(Holy Family)

		LIGHTWEIGHT		
(Crumlin)	Mick McCarthy	*beat*	Sammy Lockhart	(St John Bosco)

		LIGHT-WELTERWEIGHT		
(Immaculata)	Jim McCourt	*beat*	John Rodgers	(Lisburn)

	WELTERWEIGHT			
(Galway Olympic)	Seán Harty	*beat*	Harry Mooney	(St Matthew's)

	LIGHT-MIDDLEWEIGHT			
(Banbridge)	Eamon McCusker	*beat*	Willie Cullen	(Ballagh)

	MIDDLEWEIGHT			
(Birmingham)	Barney Burns	*beat*	Dermot McCarthy	(Crumlin)

	LIGHT-HEAVYWEIGHT			
(Port of Dublin)	Ollie Byrne	*walkover*		

	HEAVYWEIGHT			
(Coventry)	Danny McAlinden	*beat*	Jim Smith	(Avona)

DUBLIN'S OLLIE BYRNE – AN AGELESS BOXER

Dublin's Ollie Byrne was a true legend of Irish amateur boxing. In 1939 the then 13-year-old schoolboy joined the renowned St Andrew's club and he soon captured a Dublin league title at 6 stones. Ollie won his first-ever Irish title in 1948 as a junior welterweight and went on to claim six senior crowns. He represented Ireland on forty occasions, the most notable being in 1959 when he hauled himself twice off the canvas to defeat the German Karl Mildenberger – a victory that had the crowd in raptures at the National Stadium. In 1966, Mildenberger went twelve rounds with Muhammad Ali for the world heavyweight title. Having claimed his last-ever senior crown in 1967 at the age of 41, Ollie's appearance in the championships continued until 1973. In 1973, officials from the IABA, unnerved by the prospect of a 47-year-old veteran trading punches with men young enough to be his son, rejected his entry form for the senior championships. His last fight took place on 24 February 1975 at the Greenhill club's show at the Green Isle Hotel in Dublin, where he gained a split decision over Ray Heraghty, a former National Junior champion and Irish international. Ollie was a brave and skilful competitor who passed away in January 1987, aged 61.

DOWLING TO THE FORE – NATIONAL SENIOR FINALS 1968

Ollie Byrne was without doubt the most popular boxer of the night at the National Stadium on finals' night in 1968. At the age of 42, Byrne was trying to win his seventh senior title. It was not to be though as Dermot McCarthy boxed cleverly to take the middleweight title. Reigning Irish junior champion, Martin Quinn from Belfast, secured his first-ever senior title with a win over Tommy Muldoon of Coalisland in the lightweight division. Quinn was to be the surprise choice on the Irish team bound for the Mexico Olympics. The other champions chosen for Mexico were Jim McCourt, Eamon McCusker, Eddie Tracey, Brendan McCarthy and Mick Dowling, who began his record-breaking run of eight consecutive bantamweight titles with a win over John Finn.

	FLYWEIGHT			
(Arbour Hill)	Brendan McCarthy	*beat*	Freddie Lavery	(Coventry-Irish)
	BANTAMWEIGHT			
(Arbour Hill)	Mick Dowling	*beat*	John Finn	(Enterprise)
	FEATHERWEIGHT			
(Arbour Hill)	Eddie Tracey	*beat*	Paddy Devaney	(Crumlin)
	LIGHTWEIGHT			
(St John Bosco)	Marty Quinn	*beat*	Tommy Muldoon	(Coalisland)
	LIGHT-WELTERWEIGHT			
(Crumlin)	Jim McCourt	beat	Frank Downes	(St Saviour's, Dublin)
	WELTERWEIGHT			
(Dominic Savio)	Frank Young	*beat*	Seán Harty	(Coventry-Irish)
	LIGHT-MIDDLEWEIGHT			
(Banbridge)	Eamon McCusker	*beat*	Terry McCarthy	(Crumlin)
	MIDDLEWEIGHT			
(Crumlin)	Dermot McCarthy	*beat*	Ollie Byrne	(Port of Dublin)
	LIGHT-HEAVYWEIGHT			
(Edgewick)	Paddy Long	*beat*	Paddy Hughes	(Transport)
	HEAVYWEIGHT			
(Olympic, Galway)	Frank Heeney	*beat*	Martin O'Donovan	(Matt Talbot, Cork)

MICHAEL COLLINS FIGHTS LIAM NEESON

The patrons of the Royal Ballroom in Castlebar were thoroughly entertained at a cross-border boxing tournament on Sunday 24 March 1968. Chief among the bouts was a light-heavyweight clash between Belfast's Stan Corbett (father of the future Irish and Commonwealth cruiserweight champion, Darren) and Westport's future Irish international, Peter Mullen. Later, in the heavyweight bout, in a strange quirk of fate, Ballymena's Liam Neeson (the very same), showing the greater aggression and boxing ability, beat Castlebar's Michael Collins on points. Neeson would of course portray the historical figure Michael Collins in the 1995 movie of that name directed by Neil Jordan.

Neeson represented with distinction the All Saints club in Ballymena. Founded in September 1961 by Father Alex Darragh, the club celebrated its golden anniversary in 2011 with the launch of a book by legendary journalist Denis O'Hara, which narrated the history of the club. The club has produced many fine exponents of the noble art, chief among them were Maurice Dempster, John Shaw, Tony McAvoy, T.J. Hamill, Dermot Hamill and Steven Donnelly, who all brought Irish titles back to the county Antrim town. In 1993, the club's Eamon Loughran won the WBO welterweight championship. As for Neeson, in April 1964, he was unlucky to lose at the National Stadium in the semi-final of the 6st 7lb Irish schoolboys' class, while he was the runner-up in both the 1968 and 1969 Irish Juvenile Championships.

MARTY QUINN SHINES – MEXICO OLYMPIC GAMES 1968

There were to be no medals for Ireland at the Mexico Olympic Games, but perhaps the unluckiest boxer was 18-year-old Martin Quinn of the St John Bosco club in Belfast. In his opening bout in the lightweight division, Quinn disposed of Cameroon's Essomba Bernard within thirty seconds. He was then drawn against the reigning Olympic champion, Józef Grudzień of Bulgaria. Showing no fear, Quinn knocked Grudzień to the canvas in the third round, but, amid shock and confusion, went to the wrong corner as the referee waited to administer a count. The official then insisted that Quinn went to a neutral corner and it took over forty seconds for the actual count to take place. The champion recovered and went on to win on a split verdict. In the bantamweight class, Mick Dowling reached the quarterfinals after wins over East Germany's Bernard Juterzenka and the Australia's John Rakowski. However, two warnings picked up against Japan's Eli Morioka effectively denied Dowling a chance of a bronze medal.

Flyweight	Brendan McCarthy
Bantamweight	Mick Dowling
Featherweight	Eddie Tracey
Lightweight	Martin Quinn
Light-welterweight	Jim McCourt
Light-middleweight	Eamon McCusker

THREE TITLES FOR ARBOUR HILL – NATIONAL SENIOR FINALS 1969

It was a case of Arbour Hill to the fore as the Dublin club claimed three of the senior titles at the National Stadium on Friday 25 April. In the bantamweight decider, Mick Dowling put in an impressive display of power punching. In a rematch of his 1967 decider with John Finn, Dowling opened up with two rasping right-hand punches in the second round that forced the referee to intervene and end the fight. Brendan McCarthy and Eddie Treacy added to the Dublin club's tally on a night. John Gilligan of the Corinthians club took the honours in the flyweight final. As was normal at that time, the flyweight, welterweight and middleweight boxers all had to fight both their semi-finals and finals on the same evening.

	FLYWEIGHT			
(Corinthians)	John Gilligan	*beat*	Neil McLoughlin	(Derry)
	BANTAMWEIGHT			
(Arbour Hill)	Mick Dowling	*beat*	John Finn	(Tramore)
	FEATHERWEIGHT			
(Arbour Hill)	Brendan McCarthy	*beat*	Pat McAuley	(Holy Family)
	LIGHTWEIGHT			
(Arbour Hill)	Eddie Tracey	*beat*	Eddie Hendricks	(Corinthians)
	LIGHT-WELTERWEIGHT			
(Immaculata)	Jim McCourt	*beat*	Frank Murphy	(Avona)
	WELTERWEIGHT			
(Crumlin)	Frank Downes	*beat*	John Rodgers	(Lisburn)
	LIGHT-MIDDLEWEIGHT			
(Banbridge)	Eamon McCusker	*beat*	Willie Cullen	(Avona)
	MIDDLEWEIGHT			
(Tramore)	Denis O'Brien	*beat*	Dermot McCarthy	(Crumlin)
	LIGHT-HEAVYWEIGHT			
(Cookstown)	Bob Espie	*beat*	Michael Sheehan	(Limerick)
	HEAVYWEIGHT			
(Sacred Heart)	Anthony Maguire	*walkover*		

PARATROOPERS BREAK UP FIGHT IN ULSTER HALL

Soldiers of the Parachute Regiment were called into action to quell disorder in the Ulster Hall after Jim McCourt's disputed win over John Rodgers in the 1970 Ulster senior welterweight final. The row began outside the main hall as the boxers left the arena with rival supporters squaring up as acrimony over the decision boiled over. The situation became particularly nasty as mass brawls broke out in the hall's ornate foyer and lasted until two dozen paratroopers moved in to quell the unrest. Apparently, the army had been told that serious rioting had broken out in the city centre. Afterwards, an angry and bloodied Rodgers, who had been taken to hospital from the Ulster Hall in the back of an army Saracen, alleged that he had been hit with the base of the trophy. 'It is bad enough being robbed, but to get this as well!' he added.

7

THE 1970s

DERRY CLAIMS ITS FIRST SENIOR CROWN – NATIONAL SENIOR FINALS 1970

Three months after missing out on an Irish junior title, Derry's Charlie Nash sparkled as he claimed the Irish senior crown when he defeated Crumlin's Paddy Devaney on 20 March 1970. The 18-year-old silenced his critics in the National Stadium with an assured display as he out-boxed the hot favourite Devaney, a feat that earned him the 'Boxer of the Tournament' accolade. The following day, Nash was paraded around his native Derry on an open-back lorry where thousands had turned out to greet their new champion. His position as the most famous resident of Derry lasted only a matter of hours as a young girl called Rosemary Brown, better known as Dana, would win the Eurovision Song Contest in Amsterdam later that evening. The 1970 finals were explosive in many ways, with seven of the ten contests ending inside the distance. Latecomers to the stadium that evening missed Mickey Tohill's stoppage of Noel Brennan in the flyweight division. Indeed, the programme came to a somewhat premature end as Bob Espie claimed the light-heavyweight title in the second round, and Mick Collins stopped Frank Cahill in the heavyweight clash with a crisp right hand to the jaw just four minutes into their bout.

	FLYWEIGHT			
(St John Bosco)	Mickey Tohill	*beat*	Noel Brennan	(CIE)
	BANTAMWEIGHT			
(British Railways)	Mick Dowling	*beat*	Gerry Jordan	(St John Bosco)
	FEATHERWEIGHT			
(Arbour Hill)	Brendan McCarthy	*beat*	Danny Bennett	(Crumlin)
	LIGHTWEIGHT			
(St Mary's)	Charlie Nash	*beat*	Paddy Devaney	(Crumlin)
	LIGHT-WELTERWEIGHT			
(Corinthians)	Eddie Hendricks	*beat*	Tony McEvoy	(All Saints)

		WELTERWEIGHT		
(Star)	Terry McCormick	*beat*	Paddy Gilson	(Crumlin)

		LIGHT-MIDDLEWEIGHT		
(Ballyshannon)	Paddy Doherty	*beat*	Seán Harty	(St Patrick's)

		MIDDLEWEIGHT		
(British Railways)	Phil Doyle	*beat*	Frank McCormick	(Star)

		LIGHT-HEAVYWEIGHT		
(Cookstown)	Bob Espie	*beat*	Denis O'Brien	(Tramore)

		HEAVYWEIGHT		
(Irish Ropes)	Mick Collins	*beat*	Frank Cahill	(Mullinahone)

HENDRICKS STEALS THE SHOW – NATIONAL SENIOR FINALS 1971

The biggest upset at the 1971 senior finals at the National Stadium came when Eddie Hendricks of the Corinthians club retained his light-welterweight crown by defeating the highly fancied Jim Montague of Belfast. Attacking with gusto, Hendricks out-punched Montage in the second and third rounds and received a unanimous verdict from the judges. Overall, four boxers – Hendricks, Mick Dowling, Brendan McCarthy, Charlie Nash – retained their crowns in their weight divisions. Seven of the titles went to Dublin clubs.

		FLYWEIGHT		
(St Eugene's, Derry)	Neil McLaughlin	*beat*	Davy Larmour	(Albert Foundry)

		BANTAMWEIGHT		
(British Railways)	Mick Dowling	*beat*	Mickey Cullen	(CBS Wexford)

		FEATHERWEIGHT		
(Arbour Hill)	Brendan McCarthy	*beat*	Danny Bennett	(Crumlin)

		LIGHTWEIGHT		
(St Mary's)	Charlie Nash	*beat*	Ray Ross	(Ardglass)

		LIGHT-WELTERWEIGHT		
(Corinthians)	Eddie Hendricks	*beat*	Jim Montague	(Star)

		WELTERWEIGHT		
(St Saviour's, Dublin)	Frankie Downes	*beat*	John Rodgers	(Lisburn)

		LIGHT-MIDDLEWEIGHT		
(Ballyshannon)	Paddy Doherty	*beat*	Eddie Hayden	(Arbour Hill)

		MIDDLEWEIGHT		
(Crumlin)	Dermot McCarthy	*beat*	Liam Grant	(Balbriggan)

		LIGHT-HEAVYWEIGHT		
(British Railways)	Phil Doyle	*beat*	Willie Cooper	(Crumlin)

		HEAVYWEIGHT		
(British Railways)	Jack O'Rourke	*beat*	Peter Mullen	(Westport)

LONG HAIRSTYLES CONCERN IABA

The Standing Committee of the Irish Amateur Boxing Association, at its meeting on 2 May 1971, considered imposing a ban on long hairstyles as they were hindering referees in doing their job effectively. The matter was raised by the chairman of the County Dublin board, Charlie Higgins, who said that long-haired boxers posed an increasing risk for referees, since it was difficult to see cuts develop under longer fringes. Higgins reported that he had refereed a contest where a boxer had received a cut on the forehead, but it had not become apparent to him for some time. The president of the association, Mr Paddy Carroll, agreed that the issue needed to be addressed and it was referred to the chief medical officer for his opinion. By 1971, the trend among young men had moved irreversibly away from short hairstyles and, wisely, the IABA duly decided not to impose a 'short back and sides only' rule.

MARTIN HARKIN – TRAGEDY IN THE RING

Tragedy occurred in the ring in 1972. On 8 January 20-year-old Derry boxer Martin Harkin was boxing in a preliminary bout at the Ulster Junior Championships in Ballymena. His welterweight contest against Mike Docherty was stopped in the third round when Harkin received a fractured jaw. Referee Pearse McMahon called Dr Brian McHenry to the ring and the fight was stopped immediately. Harkin was taken to the Waveney Hospital in Ballymena and then transferred to Ulster Hospital in Belfast, where sadly he died on Monday 10 January. He was a member of St Mary's boxing club, Derry.

SMOKIN' JOE VOWS NEVER TO RETURN TO IRELAND

In 1971, Ireland was less than impressed when the undisputed world heavyweight champion Joe Frazier arrived with his band 'The Knockouts' to play a number of concerts. Fresh from defending his title against Muhammad Ali, Frazier's blues, funk and soul outfit had been booked to play gigs in local dance halls that were unquestionably a world removed from the bright lights of New York and Madison Square Garden. Ireland was to be the springboard for an ambitious European tour for Frazier. However, in a country where everyone was dancing nightly to the sound of the showbands, the world champion's appearances were met with indifference. Concerts in rural counties

Derry and Donegal saw 'The Knockouts' play to half-empty halls, while in Castlebar, County Mayo, barely 100 people paid into the Royal Ballroom, a venue that could hold over 4,000 patrons. With the tour bordering on a financial disaster, joint promoters Pat O'Brien and Louis Rodgers cancelled the rest of the dates. Rodgers told the media at Dublin Airport, 'The champ never wants to see Ireland again; we have been dogged by bad luck all the way.'

IRELAND *v.* ENGLAND INTERNATIONAL CANCELLED

The aftermath of the events of Sunday 30 January 1972 in Derry impacted on the Ireland *v.* England international scheduled for the National Stadium for Friday 11 February. Known as Bloody Sunday, the deaths of fourteen Civil Rights marchers at the hands of the British Army caused widespread unrest and culminated in Dublin with the burning of the British Embassy. The Irish team had included two Derry men, Charlie Nash, whose brother William was one of the marchers shot dead by soldiers, and Neil McLaughlin. The Irish and English boxing associations agreed that, 'it would be tantamount to disaster to let the match go on as scheduled'. Jim Devine of the IABA issued a statement to say that the international had been postponed indefinitely, while secretary of the English ABA, Jim Lovett, said, 'It would not have been fair to embarrass the boxers, and it might have been even worse than that.'

MCCOURT BOUNCES BACK – NATIONAL SENIOR FINALS 1972

Jim McCourt sent out an emphatic message regarding his ambition to appear at a third successive Olympic Games when he claimed his seventh Irish title by beating Jim Montague in the light-welterweight class. There was to be disappointment for McCourt in June that year when the IABA nominated Montague to represent Ireland in the light-welterweight division.

President of the IABA, Paddy Carroll, explained that the selectors felt that McCourt was too old to make an impact at the Olympics in Munich and Montague, at merely 21, deserved his chance. In the bantamweight division, Mick Dowling took his fifth successive senior crown by beating Mickey Tohill, while the surprise of the night came when Gerry Jordan of the Holy Family club stopped Phil Roche with a sweet right hook in the third round. All of the champions, together with Mickey Tohill and Jim Montague, assured themselves of a place on the Irish team bound for a tour of the United States in May that year.

	FLYWEIGHT			
(St Eugene's)	Neil McLaughlin	*beat*	Davy Larmour	(Albert Foundry)
	BANTAMWEIGHT			
(British Railways)	Mick Dowling	*beat*	Mickey Tohill	(Holy Family)
	FEATHERWEIGHT			
(Holy Family)	Gerry Jordan	*beat*	Philip Roche	(Avona)
	LIGHTWEIGHT			
(St Mary's)	Charlie Nash	*beat*	Christy McKenna	(Balbriggan)
	LIGHT-WELTERWEIGHT			
(Immaculata)	Jim McCourt	*beat*	Jim Montague	(Star)
	WELTERWEIGHT			
(Roscommon)	Terry Casey	*beat*	Seamus McGahon	(Errigal)
	LIGHT-MIDDLEWEIGHT			
(Port of Dublin)	Christy Elliott	*beat*	Terry McCarthy	(Crumlin)
	MIDDLEWEIGHT			
(Star, Belfast)	Frank McCormick	*beat*	Mick Gorman	(Corinthians)
	LIGHT-HEAVYWEIGHT			
(Irish Ropes)	Denis O'Brien	*beat*	Trevor Kerr	(Holy Family)
	HEAVYWEIGHT			
(Westport)	Peter Mullen	*beat*	Mick Collins	(Irish Ropes)

WESTPORT MAN'S BRUSH WITH GREATNESS

Ireland's clash with a United States' representative team in May 1972 saw Mayo's Peter Mullen matched against a future legend of world boxing in the shape of Larry Holmes. The international in West Orange, New Jersey, saw Irish champion Mullen meet Holmes in the heavyweight clash of a match which Ireland won by eight bouts to two. Despite a brave performance, Mullen was eventually stopped in the third round by the man who would go on to hold a version of the world heavyweight title from 1978 to 1985, making twenty successful defences in the process. Holmes had taken up boxing in his teens but had showed enough class to be chosen as a sparring partner for Muhammad Ali, Joe Frazier and Ernie Shavers.

In 2009, Mullen and Holmes met up again in New York when the Westport man travelled to the United States to watch Mayo in a Connacht football championship game at Gaelic Park. On arrival, the Mullen entourage took a bus to Easton, Pennsylvania, where they waited patiently in Holmes 'Champ's Corner' bar for the legend to appear. Peter's patience paid off when the legend duly showed up and greeted the patrons with open arms. On telling Holmes that he was from Ireland, Larry looked at Peter and said, 'I fought one Irishman –

was that you?' With hugs and slaps on the back, the two boxers spent a couple of hours sharing tales and reminiscing about their 1972 clash. Peter Mullen won the Irish heavyweight title in 1972, 1973 and 1975, and was runner-up in 1971 and 1974.

MUHAMMAD ALI *v.* AL 'BLUE' LEWIS – CROKE PARK, 19 JULY 1972

Born in 1922 in Killorgin, County Kerry, Patrick 'Butty' Sugrue made a name for himself as a circus strongman and bar owner in London. In July 1972, he found greater fame as the man who promoted Muhammad Ali's world title defence against Al 'Blue' Lewis at Croke Park in Dublin. Despite the massive hype, the fight failed to capture the imagination of local fans and took place in front of merely 20,000 spectators – an official figure that was considered to have been an exaggeration. Arriving in Dublin Airport on 12 July, Ali greeted the press by shaking a shillelagh in the air, suggesting that reigning champion Joe Frazier would soon be on the receiving end of the weapon. The top floor of Dublin's Gresham Hotel was booked solid for Ali and his entourage and they travelled each day to Oppermann's Country Club in Kilkenny to prepare for the contest. Guaranteed a cool $215,000 for the fight, Ali sparred with Joe Bugner and John Conteh each day under the watchful eye of his mother, Odessa Clay.

Two days before the fight, it was almost called off when officials discovered that the ring installed in Croke Park was smaller than the regulation 20 feet. Ireland's only ring of that size was located in the Ulster Hall and an urgent request to borrow that ring was sent north. When it duly arrived in Dublin from Belfast, it was discovered that the wrong one had been dispatched – it was in fact the juvenile ring measuring only 16 feet. At this stage, Mr Sugrue's hair may well have turned white, but an uneasy compromise was made and both men agreed that the 18-feet ring from the National Stadium be used. When news of use of the smaller ring broke, bookmakers slashed the odds on Lewis causing an upset from 25/1 to 5/1. In a departure from conservative Irish tradition, it was reported that a young and attractive Dublin girl, Betty McDermott, had been chosen to display the round numbers to spectators between rounds.

On the night itself, Ali triumphed as class prevailed. The end arrived for the challenger in the eleventh round when, bruised and tortured, he was led back to his corner by the referee. Journalist Nell McCafferty wrote that she had 'seen better fights in dancehalls in Derry'. Any profits that were made from the bill were, in theory, to be donated to 'The Handicapped Children of Ireland' charity. But, given the poor attendance – it was 15,000 short of the 'break-even' figure – Sugrue reported that the charity would receive nothing. However, Ali's visit did put Ireland on the world-boxing map again, amid the chaos on going in the North. Famously, he was pictured holding a hurling stick with Kilkenny's Eddie Keher and met the Taoiseach, Jack Lynch. A suggestion that Ali would pay a courtesy visit to President de Valera was turned down by one of the officials at Áras an Uachtaráin. The official wrote in a memorandum that it would be 'inappropriate' for a 'boastful, bombastic man' such as Ali to meet with the President.

SPLIT DECISION DENIES DOWLING – MUNICH OLYMPIC GAMES 1972

Mick Dowling's dream of an Olympic medal was dashed in his third-round tie against the reigning Olympic bantamweight champion, Cuba's Orlando Martinez. Having successfully negotiated Sweden's Ove Lunby in the first round, Dowling put in an immense display against the Cuban only to lose on a split decision. At the Games, all six of Ireland's representatives recorded victories. Jim Montague lost his second bout to the gold medallist, Ray Seales of the USA. Derry duo, Neil McLaughlin and Charlie Nash, battled to the quarterfinals, only for McLaughlin to lose to Uganda's Leo Rwabwogo, while Nash lost to the eventual gold medallist, Jan Szezepanski of Poland.

Flyweight	Neil McLaughlin
Bantamweight	Mick Dowling
Lightweight	Charlie Nash
Light-welterweight	Jim Montague
Welterweight	John Rodgers
Light-middleweight	Christy Elliott

LARMOUR'S BREAKTHROUGH – NATIONAL SENIOR FINALS 1973

After suffering two successive final defeats against his nemesis Neil McLaughlin, the Albert Foundry's Davy Larmour finally claimed an Irish senior title with a victory over Brendan Dunne (father of Bernard) in the flyweight division. It was a sweet triumph that earned Larmour a first senior appearance in an Irish vest in November that year against Romania at the National Stadium. Ireland were to go down by four bouts to two against the Eastern Europeans that night, but Larmour stole the limelight, climbing off the canvas in the second round to claim a battling victory over the fearsome Ion Sola. Ireland's only other victory that evening was none other than Brendan Dunne, who had dropped down a weight and prevailed in his light-flyweight clash with Ramos Cosma.

		FLYWEIGHT		
(Albert Foundry, Belfast)	Davy Larmour	*beat*	Brendan Dunne	(Phoenix, Dublin)
		BANTAMWEIGHT		
(Castlecomer, Kilkenny)	Mick Dowling	*beat*	Mickey Tohill	(Holy Family)
		FEATHERWEIGHT		
(St Mary's, Derry)	Damien McDermott	*beat*	Gerry Hamill	(Holy Family)
		LIGHTWEIGHT		
(St Mary's, Derry)	Charlie Nash	*beat*	Maurice Dempster	(All Saints, Ballymena)
		LIGHT-WELTERWEIGHT		
(Enniskillen)	Davy Campbell	*beat*	Noel McLaughlin	(Letterkenny)
		WELTERWEIGHT		
(Lisburn)	John Rodgers	*beat*	Eddie Hendricks	(St Saviour's, Dublin)
		LIGHT-MIDDLEWEIGHT		
(Arbour Hill)	Eddie Hayden	*beat*	Terry Riordan	(British Railways)
		MIDDLE		
(Phoenix, Dublin)	Christy Elliott	*beat*	Larry Morrison	(Garda)
		LIGHT-HEAVYWEIGHT		
(Enniskillen)	Gordon Ferris	*beat*	Paul Connolly	(Garda)
		HEAVYWEIGHT		
(Westport)	Peter Mullen	*beat*	Mick Collins	(Irish Ropes)

SAMUEL 'DAVY' LARMOUR

Davy Larmour was born in Belfast 1949 and made history by winning bronze and gold medals for Northern Ireland at successful Commonwealth Games in 1970 and 1974. In 1974, he, along with Lisburn's John Rodgers, represented Ireland in Cuba at the inaugural World Boxing Championships. Two years later, he wore the green vest at the Montreal Olympics. He turned professional soon after and in March 1983 became British bantamweight champion when he defeated Hugh Russell at the King's Hall in Belfast.

BITING STORM – IRISH JUNIOR FINALS 1973

Many years before Luis Suarez was putting the 'bite' into his opponents, the 1973 Irish juvenile finals saw a 'biting' controversy which led to the disqualification of one of the protagonists. In the 6 stone final, Glasnevin's David Tyrell complained to referee Charlie Higgins that he had been bitten on the shoulder by his opponent, Seán Johnson of the All Saints club from Ballymena. On closer inspection, the referee deemed that the mark on Tyrell's shoulder had indeed been the result of a bite and duly disqualified Johnson. Amid protests that the mark had been caused by an accident, the referee led the Ballymena boy to his corner and Tyrell was adjudged the winner. Later that evening, Brian Geoghegan from Drumshambo celebrated his fifteenth birthday in style by beating Frank Reilly of the Transport Club in the 9 stone final. In doing so, Geoghegan, whose father was in hospital recovering from an accident, earned County Leitrim its first-ever national juvenile title.

CONTROVERSY AS DAVITT WINS – NATIONAL SENIOR FINALS 1974

The Dublin and Ulster boards of the IABA were at loggerheads at the senior finals on 15 March 1974 as a controversial decision gave the featherweight title to Tommy Davitt over Gerry Hamill. After an epic encounter, all three judges had scored the contest 59-58 in Hamill's favour, but two opted to award Davitt the verdict for his overall aggression. With the mathematics defying the verdict, there was uproar in Hamill's camp as cries of 'robbery' resounded at ringside. Brendan Dunne, a clubmate of Davitt, made history by winning the first-ever light-flyweight title when he overcame a brave and battling Paddy Aspill. On the night on which Mick Dowling claimed his seventh straight bantamweight crown, Gerry Hanna of Laurencetown blasted reigning champion Dave Campbell into submission within two rounds in what was the surprise of the night. The bill also saw Neil McLaughlin return to the ring to stop Ballagh's Nick Kirwan in the flyweight final, while two Gardaí, Paul Connolly and Willie Cooper, took the light-heavyweight and heavyweight titles respectively.

		LIGHT-FLYWEIGHT		
(Phoenix)	Brendan Dunne	*beat*	Paddy Aspill	(CIE)
		FLYWEIGHT		
(St Eugene's)	Neil McLaughlin	*beat*	Noel Kirwan	(Ballagh, Wexford)
		BANTAMWEIGHT		
(Drimnagh)	Mick Dowling	*beat*	John Finn	(Tramore)
		FEATHERWEIGHT		
(Phoenix)	Tommy Davitt	*beat*	Gerry Hamill	(Holy Family)
		LIGHTWEIGHT		
(Ardglass)	Ray Ross	*beat*	Bobby Redmond	(Arbour Hill)

	LIGHT-WELTERWEIGHT			
(Laurencetown)	Gerry Hanna	*beat*	Davy Campbell	(Enniskillen)
	WELTERWEIGHT			
(Lisburn)	John Rodgers	*walkover*		
	LIGHT-MIDDLEWEIGHT			
(Arbour Hill)	Eddie Hayden	*beat*	Terry Riordan	(British Railways)
	MIDDLEWEIGHT			
(Phoenix)	Christy Elliott	*beat*	Larry Morrison	(Roscommon)
	LIGHT-HEAVYWEIGHT			
(Monaghan)	Paul Connolly	*beat*	George McClean	(Coventry)
	HEAVYWEIGHT			
(Crumlin)	Willie Cooper	*beat*	Peter Mullen	(Westport)

THE IRISH DANCING CUBANS – WORLD CHAMPIONSHIPS 1974

The inaugural World Boxing Champions, which were held in Havana, Cuba, in August 1974, saw Ireland send only two representatives, Davy Larmour and John Rodgers, together with coach Gerry Storey. Being a keen student of the sport, Storey used the trip as an opportunity to study local boxing clubs in Havana and was astounded to discover upon arrival at one gym that the young boxers were warming up by dancing to the unmistakable sound of traditional Irish music. On enquiring if he was dreaming, Storey was told that many Cuban clubs taught Irish dancing as a means of improving movement, poise and balance for young boxers. Perhaps still confused by what they had been told by Storey, Larmour was eliminated in his first bout, while Rodgers was disqualified for 'use of the head' in his second contest against Reginald Forde of Guyana.

MICK DOWLING MAKES HISTORY – NATIONAL SENIOR FINALS 1975

The star of the 1975 finals on 25 April was Mick Dowling, who won a record eighth consecutive senior bantamweight crown. In front of a packed house, the Drimnagh man outpointed Terry Hanna of the Immaculata club, an opponent whom Dowling would describe as the hardest-ever of his career. With the applause still ringing in his ears, Dowling announced his retirement from the ring, telling the crowd, 'This is the one I wanted to win and now that I have achieved it I see little point in going on.' In the lightweight bout, Charlie Nash took his fourth senior crown by beating Gerry Hamill, avenging a defeat in the

Ulster final to the Holy Family man in the process. Nash was awarded the Boxer of the Tournament accolade for his exploits while British Railways took the prize for best club.

	LIGHT-FLYWEIGHT			
(Phoenix)	Brendan Dunne	*beat*	Paddy Cox	(St Munchin's)
	FLYWEIGHT			
(Albert Foundry)	Davy Larmour	*beat*	Tony Winstone	(Glasnevin)
	BANTAMWEIGHT			
(Drimnagh)	Mick Dowling	*beat*	Terry Hanna	(Immaculata)
	FEATHERWEIGHT			
(Laurencetown)	John Feeney	*beat*	Damien McDermott	(St Mary's)
	LIGHTWEIGHT			
(St Mary's)	Charlie Nash	*beat*	Gerry Hamill	(Holy Family)
	LIGHT-WELTERWEIGHT			
(British Railways)	Christy McLoughlin	*beat*	Davy Campbell	(Enniskillen)
	WELTERWEIGHT			
(Transport)	Brian Byrne	*beat*	Eddie Hendricks	(Arbour Hill)
	LIGHT-MIDDLEWEIGHT			
(British Rail, Dublin)	Terry Riordan	*beat*	Eddie Hayden	(Arbour Hill)
	MIDDLEWEIGHT			
(Oliver Plunkett, Belfast)	Terry Young	*beat*	Eddie McDonnell	(St Francis, Limerick)
	LIGHT-HEAVYWEIGHT			
(Enniskillen)	Gordon Ferris	*beat*	Bob Nethercote	(Cookstown)
	HEAVYWEIGHT			
(Westport)	Peter Mullen	*beat*	Billy Blackwell	(Portlaoise)

HAMILL TAKES 'BEST BOXER' AWARD – NATIONAL SENIOR FINALS 1976

With places at the Montreal Olympic Games at stake, the bouts in the senior finals on Saturday 1 May were truly competitive. The star of the night was undoubtedly Waterford bantamweight John Finn who, at the eighth time of asking, finally won an Irish title, defeating Seán Russell in the process. Three champions, Brendan Dunne, Davy Larmour and Gordon Ferris, all retained their titles, while Gerry Hamill finally became Irish champion, beating Bobby Redmond on points. Hamill was awarded the Boxer of the Tournament accolade.

	LIGHT-FLYWEIGHT			
(Phoenix, Dublin)	Brendan Dunne	*beat*	Jimmy Carson	(Holy Family)
	FLYWEIGHT			
(Albert Foundry, Belfast)	Davy Larmour	*beat*	Tony Noonan	(Transport, Dublin)

		BANTAMWEIGHT		
(St Paul's, Waterford)	John Finn	*beat*	Seán Russell	(Holy Family, Belfast)

		FEATHERWEIGHT		
(Tile Hill, Coventry)	John Cooke	*beat*	Damien McDermott	(St Mary's, Derry)

		LIGHTWEIGHT		
(Holy Family)	Gerry Hamill	*beat*	Bobby Redmond	(Arbour Hill)

		LIGHT-WELTERWEIGHT		
(Crumlin, Dublin)	Christy Ruth	*beat*	Steve Early	(Coventry)

		WELTERWEIGHT		
(British Rail, Dublin)	Christy McLoughlin	*beat*	Seán McGarry	(Roscommon)

		LIGHT-MIDDLEWEIGHT		
(Transport)	Brian Byrne	*beat*	Terry Riordan	(British Railways)

		MIDDLEWEIGHT		
(Ennis)	Ollie Markham	*beat*	John Molloy	(Crumlin)

		LIGHT-HEAVYWEIGHT		
(Enniskillen)	Gordon Ferris	*beat*	Colm Forde	(Crumlin)

		HEAVYWEIGHT		
(Ballinrobe)	John McLoughlin	*beat*	Willie Cooper	(Crumlin)

LARMOUR GOES CLOSE – MONTREAL OLYMPIC GAMES 1976

The boxers in Montreal got off to the worst possible start when Gerry Hamill was outpointed in the preliminary round by the Yugoslav Ace Ruseveski. The 4–1 judges' verdict was considered to have been unfair, but the Yugoslav was a decent fighter who went on to claim a bronze medal. For welterweight Christy McLoughlin, it was to be an equally painful early exit as British star Colin Jones won their contest on a unanimous 5–0 points decision. There was no luck either for Brian Byrne when, after receiving a bye in the first stage of the light-middleweight class, he lost out to Wilfredo Guzman of Puerto Rico in the second round of the competition.

Flying the flag for Ireland was Brendan Dunne, who was victorious over the Japanese fighter Noboru Uchiyama, albeit by a technical knockout. It was an unsatisfactory ending to a fight in which Dunne had built up a slight lead, despite having been tested by his skilful opponent. During the second round, a nasty clash of heads resulted in the Japanese boxer getting a serious gash above his right eye, which prompted the referee to call for the tournament doctor. With blood gushing from the cut, the officials had no option but to stop the fight and declare Dunne the winner.

In his next bout, Dunne was to taste defeat as he came up against the eventual bronze medallist, Orlando Maldonado from Puerto Rico. Dunne lost to a superior opponent who would go on to challenge Rafael Orono unsuccessfully for the world super-bantamweight crown in 1983.

The most successful Irish boxer at Montreal was Davy Larmour, who was unlucky to lose in his quarterfinal to the eventual gold medallist, American Leo Randolph, who beat the Cuban Ramon Duvalon in the final.

Light-flyweight	Brendan Dunne
Flyweight	Davy Larmour
Lightweight	Gerry Hamill
Welterweight	Christy McLoughlin
Light-middleweight	Brian Byrne

CARSON PREVENTS WHITEWASH

Ireland's clash with England at Gloucester in February 1977 bordered on disaster with flyweight Jimmy Carson the only Irish winner as the English triumphed by ten bouts to one. Still considered a junior, Carson boxed with total maturity as he beat the tall southpaw Malcolm Gregory. On a night of mundane entertainment, Gerry Hamill's lightweight clash with Dave Williams glittered and both boxers received a standing ovation at the end. However, two public warnings picked up by Hamill swung the contest in Williams' favour. The English team that night contained Charlie Magri, who beat John Finn in the opening bout. Magri would go on to claim the WBC world flyweight title in 1983, beating Eloeoncio Mercedes at the Wembley Arena. In his debut as a professional, Magri had beaten former Irish amateur champion Neil McLaughlin. In the featherweight bout in Gloucester, Seán Doyle was stopped by Birmingham's Pat Cowdell. Cowdell, who had won a bronze medal at the 1976 Olympic Games in Montreal, would, as a professional, fight twice for the world featherweight title. His second attempt, in October 1985, ended when Azumah Nelson knocked Cowdell out cold in the first round live on terrestrial TV.

SUTCLIFFE THE STAR – NATIONAL SENIOR FINALS 1977

Irish boxing unearthed a new star in the light-flyweight class when Dubliner Philip Sutcliffe claimed honours with a superb victory over Jimmy Carson. The 17-year-old had Carson's nose bloodied in the first round such was the accuracy and volume of his punches. Sutcliffe would go on to claim bronze medals at the 1977 and 1979 European Championships and represent Ireland at the Olympic Games in 1980 and 1984. In the light-welterweight clash, champion Christy Ruth lost his title to Gerry Hanna of Laurencetown. Such was the closeness of the decision that Ruth remarked

to reporters as he left the ring, 'Call the police, there has been a robbery.'
Mel Christle took the light-heavyweight title over Artane's Barry Nugent
with his seventh first-round stoppage in a row that year.

		LIGHT-FLYWEIGHT		
(Drimnagh)	Philip Sutcliffe	beat	Jimmy Carson	(Holy Family)
		FLYWEIGHT		
(Transport, Dublin)	Tony Noonan	beat	Seán Thompson	(Transport, Dublin)
		BANTAMWEIGHT		
(St Patrick's, Wexford)	Gus Farrell	beat	John Finn	(St Paul's, Waterford)
		FEATHERWEIGHT		
(Edenderry)	Seán Brereton	beat	PJ Davitt	(Phoenix, Dublin)
		LIGHTWEIGHT		
(Holy Family)	Gerry Hamill	beat	Gerry Darcy	(Arbour Hill, Dublin)
		LIGHT-WELTERWEIGHT		
(Laurencetown, Down)	Gerry Hanna	beat	Christy Ruth	(Crumlin)
		WELTERWEIGHT		
(White City, Belfast)	Kenny Beattie	beat	Matt Cowap	(British Railways)
		LIGHT-MIDDLEWEIGHT		
(Transport)	Brian Byrne	beat	Mick Millar	(St Patrick's, Enniscorthy)
		MIDDLEWEIGHT		
(Transport, Dublin)	Terry Riordan	beat	John Molloy	(Crumlin)
		LIGHT-HEAVYWEIGHT		
(Crumlin, Dublin)	Mel Christle	beat	Barry Nugent	(Avona, Dublin)
		HEAVYWEIGHT		
(Enniskillen)	Gordon Ferris	beat	Noel Dunne	(Sunnyside, Cork)

BATTLE OF THE ALAMO SPIRIT SHOWN BY IRISH BOXERS

Ireland's boxers bounced back from an 8-1 mauling at the hands of
the USA on 17 March 1978, to claim a worthy 4-4 draw against a
Mexican-American selection in San Antonio, Texas, four days later.
Under the tutelage of Gerry Storey, the Irish team appeared in front of
6,000 fans and put on a display of heart and character which won over
the spectators. The star of the night was P.J. Davitt, whose display of
short, powerful punching stopped his accomplished opponent, David
Pastran, within two minutes of the second round. Phil Sutcliffe had
set Ireland off to a winning start in the flyweight bout, but then Gus
Farrell, Kenny Webb and Seán Brereton all lost to see Ireland trail
3-1. Davitt's win was followed by a victory for Christy Ruth over
Mike Adams at lightweight to square the match. Sugar Ray Leonard's
brother, Roger, put the USA 4-3 up with a first-round stoppage of

Brian Byrne. However, it fell to Belfast's Frank McCullagh, to in his international debut, to salvage a draw with an excellent first-round stoppage of Web Walker.

MCGUIGAN MAKES HIS MARK – NATIONAL SENIOR FINALS 1978

With Philip Sutcliffe moving up to flyweight, the tantalising prospect of his clash with the up-and-coming Hugh Russell was the main draw for the fans on Friday 7 April. The fight though was an anti-climax that lasted all of two minutes. Russell had been in control early on until Sutcliffe unleashed a lethal right hand on Russell's jaw. With his gum shield on the canvas and a split lip pouring blood, the referee wisely led Russell to his corner to avoid any more damage. Future 'Clones Cyclone' Barry McGuigan took the honours in the bantamweight class with a win over Mick Holmes of the Phoenix Club. Hopes that the Christle brothers, Terry and Joe, would claim a family double were dashed when Joe went down to Coventry's Jarlath McGough. Terry, though, made amends when he took less than a round to dispose of the Holy Family's John Ward.

	LIGHT-FLYWEIGHT			
(Transport)	Seán McDermott	*beat*	Jimmy Carson	(Holy Family)
	FLYWEIGHT			
(Drimnagh)	Philip Sutcliffe	*beat*	Hugh Russell	(Holy Family)
	BANTAMWEIGHT			
(Smithboro)	Barry McGuigan	*beat*	Mick Holmes	(Phoenix)
	FEATHERWEIGHT			
(St Patrick's, Enniscorthy)	Gus Farrell	*beat*	John Shaw	(All Saints, Ballymena)
	LIGHTWEIGHT			
(Arbour Hill)	Gerry Darcy	*beat*	Alan Doyle	(St Saviour's, Dublin)
	LIGHT-WELTERWEIGHT			
(Wexford)	Joey Fenlon	*beat*	Dougie Adams	(Corpus Christi, Belfast)
	WELTERWEIGHT			
(British Railways)	Matt Cowap	*beat*	John Thornton	(Drogheda)
	LIGHT-MIDDLEWEIGHT			
(Transport)	Brian Byrne	*beat*	Tony Heffernan	(Galway)
	MIDDLEWEIGHT			
(Crumlin)	Terry Christle	*beat*	John Ward	(Holy Family)
	LIGHT-HEAVYWEIGHT			
(Coventry)	Jarlath McGough	*beat*	Joe Christle	(Crumlin)
	HEAVYWEIGHT			
(Sunnyside, Cork)	Neilly Dunne	*beat*	John Kelleher	(Father Horgan's, Cork)

REFEREE HAS JAW BROKEN IN RING

The reign of Irish light-heavyweight champion Jarlath McGough ended abruptly in his 1979 semi-final clash with Kilkenny's Ben Lawlor. During the second round of the bout, referee Frank Bannon disqualified McGough for 'pushing' only to be met by a 'slap' from the Coventry-based boxer. Pandemonium ensued and hundreds of spectators watched as the boxer's brother, Martin, climbed through the ropes and punched the referee, breaking his jaw. Gardaí were called to the arena and the McGough brothers were taken to Kevin Street Garda station for questioning. President of the IABA Felix Jones was incandescent with rage at the turn of events, saying, 'As far as I am concerned, no more boxers from England will be allowed into these championships.'

In July that year, brothers Martin and Jarlath McGough appeared in court, charged with assaulting Bannon. The two brothers were, however, acquitted by the jury after it had been claimed that Bannon had pushed Jarlath McGough to the corner. At that point, Martin McGough, who had been injured in an earlier bout, entered the ring still in a 'concussed' and 'mentally confused state', unsure of what he was doing. His attack on the referee was considered to have been carried out while McGough was still in a dazed state.

CHARLIE NASH SUCCUMBS TO JIM WATT'S POWER

The pinnacle of Charlie Nash's professional career came on the evening of Friday 14 March 1980, when he met the WBC lightweight champion Jim Watt at Glasgow's Kelvin Hall. To say that Nash was entering the proverbial lion's den was an understatement, as 5,500 of Watt's staunchest supporters packed the arena for what was supposed to be a routine defence. Nash had claimed the European crown three months previously by beating Ken Buchanan, thus denying Scotland the prospect of a Watt versus Buchanan world-title clash in front of 50,000 at Rangers' Ibrox Park.

At 31, Nash stood on the cusp of greatness but had yet to be tested over fifteen rounds. He upset the odds in the opening round when a left-right combination sent Watt to the floor. The Scot composed himself and, by the third round, was dictating matters with vicious left hooks as Nash's eye poured with blood. The fourth round ultimately saw his downfall. As the cut worsened, Nash lost his gum shield and he was pounded to the canvas on three occasions. Referee Syd Nathan stepped in to stop proceedings, but it had been a valiant display by the Derry man.

In December 1980, Nash retained the European title against Spain's Francisco Leon at the Burlington Hotel in Dublin in a 'supper and fisticuffs' evening, where tickets cost £50 a head. Six months later, at a freezing Dalymount Park, Nash's title was relinquished to the Italian Joey Gibilisco. As Nash's career waned in north Dublin that evening, the winning debut on the undercard of Barry McGuigan was to signal the rebirth of Irish professional boxing in the 1980s.

FOSTER'S TALENT SHINES – NATIONAL SENIOR FINALS 1979

One prominent name that appeared in the programme for the 1979 finals was David McAuley of the St Anthony's club in Larne. Still to be known by his more famous Dave 'Boy' nickname, the Larne light-flyweight had champion Seán McDermott in trouble in the opening round when he sent the Dubliner to the canvas with a left hook. The champion prevailed though on a 4-1 verdict, but McAuley had done enough to convince the crowd that he would be a force to reckon with in future years. Philip Sutcliffe lost out to 17-year-old Ritchie Foster in the bantamweight final in what was an absorbing contest. Both Terry and Joe Christle claimed senior honours, with Terry defeating Limerick's Tony De Loughrey on points and Joe stopping Bob Coulter of Donaghadee in one round.

	LIGHT-FLYWEIGHT			
(Transport)	Seán McDermott	beat	Dave McAuley	(Larne)
	FLYWEIGHT			
(Holy Family)	Hugh Russell	beat	Noel Kirwan	(CBS, Wexford)
	BANTAMWEIGHT			
(Phoenix)	Richie Foster	beat	Philip Sutcliffe	(Drimnagh)
	FEATHERWEIGHT			
(Phoenix)	Mick Holmes	beat	Gus Farrell	(Enniscorthy)
	LIGHTWEIGHT			
(St Joseph's, Dublin)	Seán Doyle	beat	Martin Brereton	(Edenderry)
	LIGHT-WELTERWEIGHT			
(Phoenix, Dublin)	PJ Davitt	beat	Joey Fenlon	(CBS, Wexford)
	WELTERWEIGHT			
(White City)	Kenny Beattie	beat	John Allen	(Enniscorthy)
	LIGHT-MIDDLEWEIGHT			
(Transport)	Brian Byrne	beat	Matt Cowap	(British Railways)
	MIDDLEWEIGHT			
(Crumlin, Dublin)	Terry Christle	beat	Tony De Loughrey	(Limerick)
	LIGHT-HEAVYWEIGHT			
(Immaculata)	Frank McCullagh	beat	Ben Lawlor	(Paulstown)
	HEAVYWEIGHT			
(Crumlin, Dublin)	Joe Christle	beat	Bob Coulter	(Donaghadee)

IRELAND BEAT CANADA 9-3 IN HISTORIC FIRST MEETING

Ireland's inaugural meeting with Canada in the National Stadium on 2 November 1979 saw the home team comfortable as they eased their way to an emphatic win. At flyweight, Jimmy Carson recorded the first knockout of his career when he caught his opponent, Rick Rinneli, flush on the jaw within the opening thirty seconds. Wins followed for Philip Sutcliffe and Barry McGuigan, before P.J. Davitt was outfoxed by John Raftery in the light-welterweight clash. Ireland restored its emphatic advantage when Joe Fenelon and Ken Beattie were both awarded victories after cut eyes had forced the referee to stop proceedings. Canada's second win of the evening came when Seán O'Sullivan, whose parents hailed from Cork, won by a unanimous verdict over Willie Byrd at welterweight. Brian Byrne, Terry and Joe Christle added to Ireland's tally while Tony De Loughrey, who had only been called into the squad two days previously, was beaten in the middleweight bout.

8

THE 1980s

RECORD-BREAKING BROTHERS – NATIONAL SENIOR FINALS 1980

On Friday 7 March 1980, the Christle brothers, Terry, Joe and Mel, achieved an unprecedented treble by claiming the Irish senior titles at middleweight, heavyweight and super-heavyweight respectively. It is a record that in all probability will never be beaten. Thanks to their collective skills, the brothers carved their names indelibly into the Irish boxing history books. Terry, at middleweight, began the treble when he defeated Limerick's Tony De Loughrey in a bout that was in the balance until the third round. At that stage, Christle, a medical student at Trinity College, opened up with his cool right hand to sway the decision.

Joe Christle then faced Willie Drohan of the Arbour Hill club in the heavyweight decider. That bout lasted merely ninety seconds as two powerful right hands shook Drohan to the soles of his boxing boots. Wisely, the referee led Drohan to his corner and the crowd awaited the appearance of the third brother, Mel, for his historic moment in the super-heavyweight final. Twice in the first round of the bout, Mel sent Monaghan man Frankie Lambe to the canvas. The inevitable conclusion arrived in the second when Lambe hit the canvas for a third time and the referee was forced to administer mercy and confirm that the three Christle brothers were all Irish champions for 1980. In the other bouts that evening, Dave 'Boy' McAuley claimed the flyweight title by beating Jimmy Carson of the Holy Family club. In the bantamweight division, Richie Foster was, for the second year running, awarded the decision over Philip Sutcliffe, while Barry McGuigan's hand injury forced him to withdraw from his clash with Mick Holmes.

	LIGHT-FLYWEIGHT			
(Holy Trinity)	Gerry Hawkins	*beat*	Hugh Russell	(Holy Family)
	FLYWEIGHT			
(Larne)	Dave McAuley	*beat*	Jimmy Carson	(Holy Family)

	BANTAMWEIGHT			
(Phoenix)	Richie Foster	*beat*	Philip Sutcliffe	(Drimnagh)

	FEATHERWEIGHT	
(Phoenix, Dublin)	Mick Holmes	*walkover*

	LIGHTWEIGHT			
(St Joseph's, Dublin)	Seán Doyle	*beat*	Seán Brereton	(Edenderry)

	LIGHT-WELTERWEIGHT			
(Phoenix)	Paul Malone	*beat*	Martin Brereton	(Edenderry)

	WELTERWEIGHT			
(Phoenix)	PJ Davitt	*beat*	Joey Fenlon	(CBS, Wexford)

	LIGHT-MIDDLEWEIGHT			
(Enniscorthy)	Jim O'Sullivan	*beat*	Brian Byrne	(Transport)

	MIDDLEWEIGHT			
(Crumlin)	Terry Christle	*beat*	Tony De Loughrey	(Limerick)

	LIGHT-HEAVYWEIGHT			
(Ennis)	Mick Queally	*beat*	Ben Lawlor	(Paulstown)

	HEAVYWEIGHT			
(Crumlin, Dublin)	Joe Christle	*beat*	Willie Drohan	(Arbour Hill)

	SUPER-HEAVYWEIGHT			
(Crumlin, Dublin)	Mel Christle	*beat*	Frank Lambe	(Smithboro, Monaghan)

RUSSELL ENDS MEDAL FAMINE – MOSCOW OLYMPIC GAMES 1980

Ireland's medal famine ended at the Moscow Olympic Games when Hugh 'Little Red' Russell claimed a bronze in the flyweight division. In his quarterfinal bout with Korea's Yo Ryon Sik, Russell did enough to claim a 3-2 decision and take Ireland's first rostrum position since Tokyo in 1964. Ireland's main hope for a gold medal had been Barry McGuigan. However, the Clones featherweight had gone to the Games with an injured hand, which had caused him problems in his win over Tanzania's Issack Mabushi. The injury had affected McGuigan's preparations – both physical and mental – and, with his hand frozen by injections, he was to lose 4-1 to Winfred Kabunda in his next bout. Both McGuigan and Russell would turn professional under Barney Eastwood in Belfast within a year.

Light-flyweight	Gerry Hawkins
Flyweight	Hugh Russell
Bantamweight	Phil Sutcliffe
Featherweight	Barry McGuigan
Lightweight	Seán Doyle
Light-welterweight	Martin Brereton
Welterweight	P.J. Davitt

THE LONELY DEATH OF AN IRISH PROMOTER

The death of Gerald Egan in December 1980 saw the passing of one of Ireland's most colourful boxing promoters. In the 1940s, Egan began his career by overseeing bills at Dalymount and Tolka parks that attracted huge crowds from all over Ireland. Among the stars of the ring to appear on Egan's bills were Jimmy Ingle, John 'Spike' McCormick, Pat Mulcahy, Chris Cole and Belfast's Tommy Armour. He was a natural entrepreneur who brought Primo Carnera to Dublin for an exhibition. It was his friendship with Jack Doyle that made him famous all over Europe, promoting many of his fights in the closing part of the boxer's career. He acted as groomsman to Doyle when he married the actress Movita Castaneda in Dublin in 1943, an occasion that drew thousands on to the streets outside the Westland Row church. Jimmy Ingle recalled of Egan, 'At a time when Dublin needed entertainment, Egan provided it and gave many young Irish boxers the opportunity to fight in front of our own people.' Born in Cork in 1919, Gerard Egan died sadly and tragically in a fire at a men's hostel in London.

SEVEN TITLES GO NORTH – NATIONAL SENIOR FINALS 1981

There was anticipation in the air as Olympic medallist Hugh Russell met Dave 'Boy' McAuley in the 1981 flyweight final. Reigning champion McAuley, who had been overlooked for the flyweight berth at the Moscow Olympics, felt he had a point to prove over Russell. McAuley, with a slight advantage in height and reach, tried to take the fight to southpaw Russell, but the Belfast man was the snappier puncher and staggered his opponent midway through the second round as he recorded a clear victory.

Russell's clubmate Roy Webb underlined his impressive pedigree by stopping former light-flyweight champion Seán McDermott in the second round. At lightweight, an explosive knockout was delivered with power and precision as Damien Fryers stopped his clubmate Dougie Adams within one minute. Fryers took the contest to Adams from the first bell and set him up perfectly for a telling punch which left his opponent poleaxed on the canvas. Paddy Finn fought off the brave challenge of Noel Dunne to capture the super-heavyweight title. Dunne took two counts in the second round and was given a public warning for use of the head in the third, as Finn's power proved too much for the Cork man. Belfast's Holy Trinity was awarded the club of the tournament accolade.

	LIGHT-FLYWEIGHT			
(Rosemount, Derry)	Gerry Duddy	*walkover*		

	FLYWEIGHT			
(Holy Family)	Hugh Russell	*beat*	Dave McAuley	(St Agnes, Belfast)

	BANTAMWEIGHT			
(Holy Family)	Roy Webb	*beat*	Seán McDermott	(Transport)

	FEATHERWEIGHT			
(Transport)	Gerry Delaney	*beat*	Seán Hanna	(Oliver Plunkett, Belfast)

	LIGHTWEIGHT			
(Holy Trinity)	Damien Fryers	*beat*	Dougie Adams	(Holy Trinity)

	LIGHT-WELTERWEIGHT			
(Oliver Plunkett, Belfast)	Dave McAllister	*beat*	Denis Horgan	(London)

	WELTERWEIGHT			
(White City)	Kenny Beattie	*beat*	John De Loughrey	(St John's, Limerick)

	LIGHT-MIDDLEWEIGHT			
(Holy Trinity)	Ray Bell	*beat*	Brian Byrne	(Transport)

	MIDDLEWEIGHT			
(St Mary's, Dublin)	Terry Mahony	*beat*	John Fitzgerald	(Letterkenny)

	LIGHT-HEAVYWEIGHT			
(Enniscorthy)	Jim O'Sullivan	*beat*	Mick Queally	(Ennis)

	HEAVYWEIGHT			
(St John's, Limerick)	Jim Ingalls	*beat*	Bob Coulter	(Ledley Hall, Belfast)

	SUPER-HEAVYWEIGHT			
(Donore, Dublin)	Paddy Finn	*beat*	Noel Dunne	(Sunnyside, Cork)

BRITISH HEAVYWEIGHT TITLE FOR ENNISKILLEN

Four-time Irish senior champion, Gordon Ferris from Enniskillen, claimed the British heavyweight title when he defeated Liverpool's Billy Aird at the Aston Villa Sports Centre on Monday 30 March 1981. At 27 years of age, Ferris took the decision on the narrowest of margins over fifteen rounds against an opponent who had spent over £1,300 ferrying his supporters to the fight. With a technique that was described as 'more suited to a pub car park than a boxing ring', Aird was warned numerous times by referee Harry Gibbs for his unorthodox tactics. A storming last five rounds gave a tiring Ferris the verdict and he was presented with the coveted Lonsdale Belt.

After the fight, 35-year-old Aird announced his retirement from the ring, while a joyful Ferris had to contemplate a bout with challenger Neville Meade within sixty days. That fight, however, did not take place until 12 October. It was to be a bad night for the Irishman as Meade, a Swansea-based Jamaican, took merely two minutes to connect with a right hand that sent Ferris to the canvas. The sound of Ferris' head meeting the canvas reverberated around the packed hall. At 34, Meade became the oldest British heavyweight champion and, at 16st 3lb, one of the heaviest champions ever. Undeterred, Ferris fought a further four times, winning on three occasions, and retired in June 1982 after losing to David Pearce in a final eliminator for a crack at Meade's crown.

DE LOUGHREY FINALLY CLAIMS CROWN – NATIONAL SENIOR FINALS 1982

On a night of shocks, Limerick middleweight Tony De Loughrey finally captured a senior title by beating Johnny Thompson in the middleweight final. In a dull bout, De Loughrey was the more impressive boxer and kept Thompson under pressure throughout. Ken Beattie was the only man to retain his title when he put in a superb performance to outpoint Denis Horgan at welterweight. Paul Fitzgerald, who earlier that season had captured the national junior title, made it a notable double when he captured the senior title by beating Tommy Tobin. Ulster took six of the twelve titles, but two internationals, Gerry Hawkins and Damien Fryers, were surprisingly beaten. Other favourites to fall were Martin Brereton and Jim Ingalls.

There was a certain amount of controversy surrounding the lightweight final, as many people were surprised when the judges gave a split decision to Patsy Ormonde over reigning champion Damien Fryers. It was a most explosive affair, with both boxers throwing punches from all angles and distances right from the first bell. Seán and Martin Brereton found themselves faced with a problem after the quarterfinals. Their respective victories over Frank Connolly and Jim Toye meant that the brothers would meet in the semi-finals. After a dressing room discussion, it was agreed that Martin would go through to the final, where he lost out to David Irving.

	LIGHT-FLYWEIGHT			
(Beechmount, Belfast)	Alex O'Neill	*beat*	Gerry Hawkins	(Holy Trinity)
	FLYWEIGHT			
(Rosemount, Derry)	Gerry Duddy	*beat*	Seán McDermott	(Transport, Dublin)
	BANTAMWEIGHT			
(Arklow)	Paul Fitzgerald	*beat*	Tommy Tobin	(Irish Ropes, Kildare)
	FEATHERWEIGHT			
(Transport)	Shay Thompson	*walkover*		
	LIGHTWEIGHT			
(Donore)	Patsy Ormond	*beat*	Damien Fryers	(Holy Trinity)

		LIGHT-WELTERWEIGHT		
(Holy Trinity)	David Irving	*beat*	Martin Brereton	(Edenderry)
		WELTERWEIGHT		
(White City, Belfast)	Kenny Beattie	*beat*	Denis Horgan	(London)
		LIGHT-MIDDLEWEIGHT		
(Clonoe, Tyrone)	Tommy Corr	*beat*	Des Brackett	(Oxford)
		MIDDLEWEIGHT		
(St John's, Limerick)	Tony De Loughrey	*beat*	Johnny Thompson	(Derry)
		LIGHT-HEAVYWEIGHT		
(Holy Family, Drogheda)	John Thornton	*beat*	John Flynn	(Roscommon)
		HEAVYWEIGHT		
(Enniscorthy)	Jim O'Sullivan	*beat*	Jim Ingalls	(St John's, Limerick)
		SUPER-HEAVYWEIGHT		
(Letterkenny)	Eamonn Coyle	*beat*	Eamonn Quinn	(Ardnaree, Mayo)

REFEREE ALMOST ACCUSED OF MURDER

On 5 October 1982, Belfast's Hugh Russell and Davy Larmour clashed at the Ulster Hall for the Irish bantamweight title. The fight, which was also a final eliminator for the British title, was a truly bloody affair that went the full fifteen rounds. Russell was awarded the narrowest of decisions by referee Mike Jacobs in a ring that resembled a butcher's shambles. On returning to London, Jacobs left his white shirt to be dry-cleaned. However, when he returned to collect it he was handed a note on behalf of local police asking him to report to the station. Once there, Jacobs was asked how his shirt had come to be covered in so much blood. A simple explanation that he had refereed a boxing match in Belfast duly resolved the matter with the police. It seemed that the owner of the dry-cleaners had become suspicious when he was handed the shirt and phoned police. He was convinced that Jacobs had been involved in a knife murder.

THREE TITLES GO BY WALKOVER – NATIONAL SENIOR FINALS 1983

Flyweight Gerry Duddy and Arklow bantamweight Paul Fitzgerald successfully defended their titles, while Tony De Loughrey stepped up from middleweight to take the light-heavy crown by defeating Gerry Storey junior. Reigning champion Patsy Ormond, who had moved from lightweight to light-welterweight, found Wexford's Billy Walsh too hot to handle and was comprehensively outpointed. Three of the twelve titles were taken on walkovers. Gerry Hawkins was the only entry in the light-flyweight division, while Sam Storey, a flu victim, conceded a walkover to Tyrone's Tommy Corr. English-born Tony Hallett took the super-heavyweight title in the absence through injury of Cathal Ryan. The only stoppage of the night was recorded by De Loughrey when he caught the elder of the Storey brothers, Gerry, with a southpaw left. He followed that up with a sweeping right in the second round which landed flush on Storey's jaw and the Belfast boxer went down for the full count. The welterweight final was also a lively affair as Kieran Joyce maintained an unbeaten record for the season with a deserved points victory over former champion Joe Fenlon from Wexford.

	LIGHT-FLYWEIGHT			
(Holy Trinity)	Gerry Hawkins	*walkover*		
	FLYWEIGHT			
(Rosemount, Derry)	Gerry Duddy	*beat*	Alex O'Neill	(Holy Trinity)
	BANTAMWEIGHT			
(Arklow)	Paul Fitzgerald	*beat*	Tommy Tobin	(Irish Ropes, Kildare)
	FEATHERWEIGHT			
(Holy Family)	Roy Webb	*beat*	Noel Hickey	(Glasnevin)
	LIGHTWEIGHT			
(Holy Family)	Tony Dunlop	*beat*	Paul Larkin	(Transport)
	LIGHT-WELTERWEIGHT			
(St Joseph's, Wexford)	Billy Walsh	*beat*	Patsy Ormond	(Donore)
	WELTERWEIGHT			
(Sunnyside, Cork)	Kieran Joyce	*beat*	Joey Fenlon	(CBS, Wexford)
	LIGHT-MIDDLEWEIGHT			
(Clonoe, Tyrone)	Tommy Corr	*walkover*		
	MIDDLEWEIGHT			
(Crumlin)	Brian Byrne	*beat*	Jack Thompson	(Holy Family)
	LIGHT-HEAVYWEIGHT			
(Limerick)	Tony De Loughrey	*beat*	Gerry Storey	(Holy Family)
	HEAVYWEIGHT			
(Mullinahone)	Noel Guiry	*beat*	Seamus McDonagh	(Enfield)
	SUPERHEAVYWEIGHT			
(Newcastle)	Tony Hallet	*walkover*		

IRELAND WHITEWASH THE SCOTS IN KUTTNER SHIELD

Ireland's class of 1983 emulated the team of 1967 by putting the Scots to the sword in April 1983 in the annual international for the Kuttner Shield. The 10-0 result against a somewhat under-strength Scots team was fought in a sparsely filled National Stadium. Billy Walsh was the only home boxer to be tested by the opposition. It was a night on which two Drogheda boxers excelled, with Johnny Kilroy winning his featherweight clash against Albert Ewan, while Antonio Floody outclassed Paul Munroe at light-welterweight. On 10 March 1967, Ireland had recorded its first international whitewash when the Scots left Dublin on the wrong end of a 10-0 hammering. The fight of the night in 1967 saw Eamon McCusker avenge a knockout he had suffered against ABA and Commonwealth champion Tom Imrie with a stunning display of powerful boxing in the light-middleweight fight.

STEVE COLLINS LOSES TO NOEL MAGEE – NATIONAL SENIOR FINALS 1984

Future WBO super-middleweight world champion Steve Collins met Belfast's Noel Magee in the fight of the night at the 1984 finals and was unlucky to lose on a 3-2 majority decision. Magee's aggression was the decisive factor as he kept coming forward, taking the fight to Collins. The Dubliner was more accurate with his punches, but did not throw enough to convince the judges. Gerry Hawkins took just forty seconds to end the light-flyweight final when he knocked out Mark Owens. The bantamweight final was the expected thriller with a vintage display from Phil Sutcliffe, who outpointed Derry's Roy Nash. Sam Storey was an easy points winner over Paddy Ruth in the light-middleweight final. Ruth was floored by a peach of a left hook midway through the first round and Storey's superiority was never in doubt. Jim O'Sullivan captured the heavyweight title when he outpointed Jim Ingalls in a scrappy affair.

	LIGHT-FLYWEIGHT			
(Holy Trinity)	Gerry Hawkins	*beat*	Mark Owens	(St Mary's, Derry)
	FLYWEIGHT			
(Rock, Derry)	Seán Casey	*beat*	Derek Zambra	(Donore)
	BANTAMWEIGHT			
(Drimnagh)	Philip Sutcliffe	*beat*	Roy Nash	(St Mary's, Derry)
	FEATHERWEIGHT			
(Arklow)	Paul Fitzgerald	*beat*	Tommy Tobin	(Irish Ropes)
	LIGHTWEIGHT			
(Transport)	Paul Larkin	*beat*	Seán McCormack	(Newhill)
	LIGHT-WELTERWEIGHT			
(Wexford)	Billy Walsh	*beat*	Barry Joyce	(Sunnyside, Cork)
	WELTERWEIGHT			
(Sunnyside, Cork)	Kieran Joyce	*beat*	Brendan O'Hara	(St George's)
	LIGHT-MIDDLEWEIGHT			
(Holy Family)	Sam Storey	*beat*	Paddy Ruth	(Drimnagh)

	MIDDLEWEIGHT			
(CIE)	John Phoenix	*beat*	Tommy Corr	(Clonoe, Tyrone)

	LIGHT-HEAVYWEIGHT			
(Sacred Heart)	Noel Magee	*beat*	Steve Collins	(St Saviour's)

	HEAVYWEIGHT			
(Enniscorthy)	Jim O'Sullivan	*beat*	Jim Ingalls	(Limerick)

	SUPER-HEAVYWEIGHT			
(Donore)	Joe Egan	*beat*	Christy Ryan	(Drimnagh)

FRUSTRATION YET AGAIN – LOS ANGELES OLYMPICS 1984

Both Gerry Hawkins and Philip Sutcliffe were chosen to represent Ireland in their second Olympic Games as Ireland sent a team of six boxers to Los Angeles. However, their journey to the United States was not a happy one as freak cloudbursts saw them diverted from New York to Boston, where they sat for five hours before it was decided that an overnight stay was necessary. The following day the squad flew to Lake Placid to begin intensive acclimatisation treatment. For the first time, head guards were used in the Olympic tournaments and Ireland was out of luck as Hawkins was eliminated by silver medallist Salvadore Todisco in his opening bout. At bantamweight, Sutcliffe lost unanimously to eventual gold medallist Maurizio Stecca in the first round. Paul Fitzgerald was successful in his opening two contests, but lost narrowly to Uganda's Charles Lubulwa for a place in the quarterfinals. Kieran Joyce, who stopped Basil Boniface in his first outing, was subsequently eliminated by Finland's Johi Nyman, while Tommy Corr lost out in his second outing to gold medallist Jun Sup Shin. Sam Storey, who had been unwell in the run-up to the competition, was eliminated by Italy's Romolo Casamonica.

Light-flyweight	Gerry Hawkins
Bantamweight	Philip Sutcliffe
Featherweight	Paul Fitzgerald
Welterweight	Kieran Joyce
Light-middleweight	Sam Storey
Middleweight	Tommy Corr

JOHNNY MCQUADE – STREET-FIGHTING MAN FROM THE SHANKILL ROAD

The death, on 19 November 1984, of 72-year-old Johnny McQuade saw the passing of one of Belfast's most colourful characters. A staunch supporter of the Revd Ian Paisley, McQuade was elected to the House

of Commons in 1979 as the DUP representative for North Belfast.
A former soldier, docker and boxer, McQuade was prone to offering his
political opponents to 'come outside' to settle arguments with their fists.
As an amateur, he appeared in a tournament in the National Stadium in
November 1941, losing by knockout to Gerry Kilcullen in the second
round. McQuade's display was reported thus, 'For the second week in a
row, G. Kilcullen, the promising lightweight, met with poor opposition in
Belfast's J. McQuade, a somewhat ancient and heavily tattooed warrior
who had plenty of experience but little else.' His professional career –
fought under the name Jack Higgins – was equally as mundane. McQuade
is well remembered in political circles for his malapropisms and in folklore
was once said to have claimed that 'the IRA is like an octopus, spreading
its eight testicles across Northern Ireland'.

KIERAN JOYCE SHINES AS IRELAND LOSE 6-4 TO ENGLAND

Kieran Joyce from Cork's Sunnyside Club, well known for his aggressive
style in the ring, was the star performer of the night as Ireland lost
to England in the National Stadium on Friday 23 November 1984.
Matched against Rod Douglas at light-middleweight, Joyce impressed
the judges with a storming third round to win the bout on a split
decision. Other winners for Ireland on the night included Alan Keogh,
Roy Nash and Noel Reid. With Ireland trailing 5-4, Donore's Joe
Egan's opportunity to claim a draw was thwarted when he was stopped
by Guy Williamson in the heavyweight fight.

Kieran Joyce won his first Irish title aged 18 in 1983. He represented
Ireland at both the 1984 and 1988 Olympic Games and claimed a bronze
medal at the 1983 European Championships in Bulgaria. In 2007, Joyce,
together with Gerry Storey and Billy Walsh, were inducted into the
IABA's Hall of Fame. His opponent in Dublin in 1984, Rod Douglas,
turned professional in 1987 and was stopped by Herol Graham in a
British middleweight title fight in 1989. Douglas underwent brain surgery
to remove a clot after that fight and retired from boxing.

'THAT' GLORY NIGHT AT LOFTUS ROAD

On Saturday 8 June 1985, a massive crowd of 27,000 fans descended
on London's Loftus Road to see Barry McGuigan challenge the holder
Eusebio Pedroza for the WBA featherweight title. The champion was
a boxing legend, having held the crown since 1978, and the fight was

a classic. McGuigan caught Pedroza with a sweet right hand in the seventh round that floored the Panamanian. However, the fight went the distance and the decision went deservedly to McGuigan. The scenes that followed were unforgettable as the Irish fans celebrated wildly in London, Dublin, Belfast, Clones and beyond. The fight was the most-watched sporting event on BBC television in 1985 and, in December, 'The Clones Cyclone' was voted BBC Sports Personality of the Year.

HOUSE FIRE DAMPENS MCGUIGAN'S BIG NIGHT

The people of Clones danced and sang long into the night to celebrate their most famous son's world title victory in June 1985. However, with dawn breaking and the streets emptying of partygoers, the sound of a fire engine rushing through a Monaghan morning caught the attention of many. The cries of Brid Rooney, a relative of the McGuigans, were heard coming from a window above the family shop and alerted people that there was a fire raging within. Mrs Rooney was rescued, but considerable damage had been caused to the McGuigan family home, which was to the rear of the shop. Both Barry and his father Pat were of course in London while the drama unfolded. However, they were assured by Barry's mother, Kate, that there was no need to return home early. The fire was a miserable end to what had been one of Clones' most memorable nights, a night that had seen many fans travel to the Monaghan town to watch the fight and savour the atmosphere. The town had been packed and the bars stayed open into the small hours, screening endless re-runs of the contest. Despite the excitement, Kate McGuigan had confined herself to a bedroom for the duration of the bout. She sat praying as the voice of Luciano Pavarotti drowned out the noise from the streets.

STOREY SHADES WIN OVER COLLINS – NATIONAL SENIOR FINALS 1985

The 1985 senior finals saw the Sutcliffe brothers from Drimnagh in action yet again. Phil successful outpointed Bob McCarthy in the bantamweight final, while Derek had to retire with a cut eye in the third round of his featherweight bout. However, the decision went the judges, who gave him a unanimous verdict over Bob McCarthy. Seán Casey retained the flyweight title with a split decision over double Olympian and reigning champion, Gerry Hawkins. Rising star Damien Denny won his fight when he forced defending titleholder Billy Walsh into submission in the second round. Walsh had been caught by a neat right to the head early in the round and the referee gave him a standing count. Thereafter, he was in all sorts of trouble as Denny piled on the pressure. Neil Duddy, a younger brother of former international Gerry, impressed in the flyweight final against Michael Thompson. In the middleweight final, Sam Storey proved his class when he recorded a victory over Steve Collins of the St Saviour's club.

	LIGHT-FLYWEIGHT			
(Phoenix, Derry)	Neil Duddy	*beat*	Michael Thompson	(Transport)
	FLYWEIGHT			
(Rock, Derry)	Seamus Casey	*beat*	Gerry Hawkins	(Holy Trinity)
	BANTAMWEIGHT			
(Drimnagh)	Philip Sutcliffe	*beat*	Roy Nash	(St Mary's, Derry)
	FEATHERWEIGHT			
(Drimnagh, Dublin)	Derek Sutcliffe	*beat*	Bobby McCarthy	(Donore)
	LIGHTWEIGHT			
(Holy Family)	Brendan Lowe	*beat*	Peter Murphy	(Drimnagh)
	LIGHT-WELTERWEIGHT			
(Holy Trinity)	Damien Denny	*beat*	Billy Walsh	(Wexford)
	WELTERWEIGHT			
(Manchester)	John Reid	*beat*	Brendan O'Hara	(St George's, Belfast)
	LIGHT-MIDDLEWEIGHT			
(Sunnyside, Cork)	Kieran Joyce	*beat*	Paddy Ruth	(Drimnagh, Dublin)
	MIDDLEWEIGHT			
(Holy Family)	Sam Storey	*beat*	Steve Collins	(St Saviour's, Dublin)
	LIGHT-HEAVYWEIGHT			
(Paulstown)	Ger Lawlor	*beat*	Dan Curran	(Sealink, Dublin)
	HEAVYWEIGHT			
(Enniscorthy)	Jim O'Sullivan	*beat*	Tony Hallett	(Blakelaw, Newcastle)
	SUPER-HEAVYWEIGHT			
(Kirby, Liverpool)	Brendan Deasy	*beat*	Joe Egan	(Donore, Dublin)

GREAT NIGHT FOR GORDON JOYCE – NATIONAL SENIOR FINALS 1986

A capacity crowd saw light-welterweight Gordon Joyce add the senior light-welterweight title to the junior title, which he had won earlier in the season. He was followed into the ring by his brother Kieran, who defended his middleweight crown in style against John Reid. Philip Sutcliffe, seeking the fifth senior title his career, was beaten in the bantamweight final by the assured John Lowey. Defending champion Sutcliffe used up all his experience in trying to subdue Lowey, but the Ledley Hall boxer was calm and collected as he picked off his punches to great effect to wrap up a unanimous decision. Ballyclare's Johnston Todd proved too powerful for Dubliner Michael Thompson when he stopped him inside a round. Tallaght featherweight David Hughes was in trouble early on when Bobby McCarthy dropped him with a left hook after thirty seconds. Hughes fought back skilfully and by the last round he had done enough to claim a unanimous verdict from all five judges.

	LIGHT-FLYWEIGHT			
(Ballyclare)	Johnston Todd	*beat*	Michael Thompson	(Transport)
	FLYWEIGHT			
(Darndale, Dublin)	Joe Lawlor	*beat*	Paul Buttimer	(Sunnyside, Cork)
	BANTAMWEIGHT			
(Ledley Hall, Belfast)	John Lowey	*beat*	Philip Sutcliffe	(Drimnagh, Dublin)
	FEATHERWEIGHT			
(St Mary's)	David Hughes	*beat*	Bobby McCarthy	(Donore)
	LIGHTWEIGHT			
(Irish Ropes, Kildare)	Tommy Tobin	*beat*	Michael Carruth	(Drimnagh)
	LIGHT-WELTERWEIGHT			
(Sunnyside, Cork)	Gordon Joyce	*beat*	Peter Murphy	(Drimnagh)
	WELTERWEIGHT			
(Holy Trinity)	Damien Denny	*beat*	Billy Walsh	(St Joseph's, Wexford)
	LIGHT-MIDDLEWEIGHT			
(Sunnyside, Cork)	Kieran Joyce	*beat*	John Reid	(Manchester)
	MIDDLEWEIGHT			
(St Saviour's, Dublin)	Steve Collins	*beat*	Henry Byrne	(Sarsfield, Limerick)
	LIGHT-HEAVYWEIGHT			
(St Patrick's, Enniscorthy)	Jim O'Sullivan	*beat*	Ger Lawlor	(Paulstown)
	HEAVYWEIGHT			
(Southill/Army)	Tony De Loughrey	*beat*	Noel Guiry	(Mullinahone)
	SUPER-HEAVYWEIGHT			
(Antrim)	Alan Owens	*beat*	John Magee	(Tramore)

HUGH 'LITTLE RED' RUSSELL

Born in 1959, Hugh Russell won a Commonwealth Games medal in Edmonton in 1978 and became Ireland's first Olympic medallist in sixteen years when he took bronze in the flyweight class in 1980. Known as 'Little Red', Russell turned professional in 1981 and won two British titles at bantamweight and then flyweight. He was the first boxer to win a British title at both divisions in that order. In October 1982 he defeated Davy Larmour at the Ulster Hall to win the Irish Bantamweight title. The fight was also a final eliminator for the British bantamweight title. In January 1983, he appeared in the last fifteen-round British title fight against reigning bantamweight champion, John Feeney. The fight was stopped in the thirteenth round when the referee disqualified Feeney. Russell lost his title in a rematch with Davy Larmour in the King's Hall six weeks later and decided to drop a weight to flyweight. In 1984, he defeated Kelvin Smart to take the British title and defended it twice to win the Lonsdale Belt outright.

AN OLD-SCHOOL GARDA

Jim 'Branno' Brannigan served the Garda Síochána with distinction from 1931 until his retirement in 1973. However, his association with, and service to, amateur boxing was long and proud. His death in 1986 saw the passing of a truly epic figure. Born in 1910, Brannigan began a lifelong association with boxing on joining the police and won the Leinster heavyweight title in 1936 when he defeated Tom Penny of the St Andrew's ABC. A cartoon, which exaggerated the size of the champion's ears, appeared in a local paper and Brannigan was afforded the nickname 'Lugs' by locals. It was a nickname that irritated him greatly.

Brannigan was a policeman who took no prisoners in the ring, or on the streets. He commanded respect and fear in equal quantities. As former Irish presidential candidate Senator David Norris recalled, 'As a university student I recall seeing Garda "Lugs" Brannigan in the Olympic Ballroom. He parted the hordes like the Dead Sea to take three people who were in front of the bandstand into the back alley and rendered his own justice.' He was an old-fashioned cop who believed that a clip round the ear taught more lessons than appeasement. His long service to the IABA saw him as official, referee and judge until his later years. On 12 October 1966, the Detective Sergeant refereed non-stop in the National Stadium for almost four hours at the Dublin vocational schools' championships, overseeing thirty-three successive bouts. It was estimated that Jim had refereed over 15,000 fights throughout his career. He retired from the boxing scene in 1983 and moved to Summerhill, County Meath, where he died in 1986.

RAY CLOSE TAKES THE PLAUDITS – NATIONAL SENIOR FINALS 1987

A capacity crowd at the National Stadium saw the Joyce brothers from Cork score another family double in the finals, with Kieran powering his way to victory over Kevin Lynch, while Gordon finished strongly to retain his title against Belfast's Brendan Lowe. The Sunnyside club claimed a third title on the night when Paul Buttimer beat Joe Lawlor in a superb flyweight final. It was also a special night for Enniscorthy light-heavyweight Jim O'Sullivan, who won his seventh senior title, making it three at heavyweight, three at light-heavyweight and one at light-middleweight. He comprehensively outpointed former world light-middleweight bronze medallist Tommy Corr. Paul Fitzgerald made a winning return to the Irish scene with a unanimous points victory over John Kilroy in the featherweight decider. Fitzgerald, who was based in the United States, was too sharp for Kilroy, who battled bravely in the hope of catching the Arklow man. The award for 'Outstanding Boxer of the Championships' went to Ray Close of the Ledley Hall club in Belfast.

		LIGHT-FLYWEIGHT		
(St Munchin's, Limerick)	P.J. O'Halloran	*beat*	Ray Gifford	(St Pappin's, Dublin)
		FLYWEIGHT		
(Sunnyside, Cork)	Paul Buttimer	*beat*	Joe Lawlor	(Darndale, Dublin)
		BANTAMWEIGHT		
(Ring, Derry)	Roy Nash	*beat*	John Lowey	(Ledley Hall, Belfast)
		FEATHERWEIGHT		
(Transport)	Paul Fitzgerald	*beat*	John Kilroy	(Holy Family, Drogheda)
		LIGHTWEIGHT		
(Drimnagh)	Michael Carruth	*beat*	Sylvie Furlong	(St Michael's, Wexford)
		LIGHT-WELTERWEIGHT		
(Sunnyside, Cork)	Gordon Joyce	*beat*	Brendan Lowe	(Holy Trinity)
		WELTERWEIGHT		
(St Joseph's, Wexford)	Billy Walsh	*beat*	Damien Denny	(Holy Trinity)
		LIGHT-MIDDLEWEIGHT		
(Sunnyside, Cork)	Kieran Joyce	*beat*	Kevin Lynch	(Phoenix, Dublin)
		MIDDLEWEIGHT		
(Ledley Hall, Belfast)	Ray Close	*beat*	Paddy Ruth	(Drimnagh)
		LIGHT-HEAVYWEIGHT		
(St Patrick's, Enniscorthy)	Jim O'Sullivan	*beat*	Tommy Corr	(Clonoe, Tyrone)
		HEAVYWEIGHT		
(Donore, Dublin)	Joe Egan	*beat*	Dan Curran	(British Railways)
		SUPER-HEAVYWEIGHT		
(Ballyclare)	Willie Clyde	*beat*	John Magee	(Tramore)

WAYNE TO THE FORE – NATIONAL SENIOR FINALS 1988

The Joyce brothers, Kieran and Gordon, were pushed to the extreme in the 1988 senior finals but both retained their titles by the narrowest margins possible. However, the victory of Gordon over Antonio Floody of Drogheda was greeted by loud protests from the capacity crowd who felt that the Louth man had done enough to win the fight. P.J. O'Halloran at light-flyweight, Paul Buttimer at flyweight and Roy Nash at bantamweight all lost their titles. Belfast's rising star Wayne McCullough impressed as he claimed his first senior title, seeing off Limerick-based P.J. O'Halloran. In the third round, McCullough increased the pace of the fight and a sweeping left hand staggered O'Halloran, who was on borrowed time thereafter. The referee stopped the fight two minutes into the round. Joe Lawlor sealed the flyweight title with a sweet victory over Paul Buttimer, the man who had defeated him in 1987. Southpaw Roy Nash tried bravely to take the fight to John Lowey in the bantamweight clash, but was left frustrated as Lowey picked him off with accurate punches with both hands.

	LIGHT-FLYWEIGHT			
(Albert Foundry)	Wayne McCullough	*beat*	P.J. O'Halloran	(Limerick)
	FLYWEIGHT			
(Darndale)	Joe Lawlor	*beat*	Paul Buttimer	(Sunnyside, Cork)
	BANTAMWEIGHT			
(Ledley Hall)	John Lowey	*beat*	Roy Nash	(Ring, Derry)
	FEATHERWEIGHT			
(Transport)	Paul Fitzgerald	*beat*	John Kilroy	(Holy Family, Drogheda)
	LIGHTWEIGHT			
(Drimnagh)	Michael Carruth	*beat*	Sylvie Furlong	(St Michael's, Wexford)
	LIGHT-WELTERWEIGHT			
(Sunnyside, Cork)	Gordon Joyce	*beat*	Antonio Floody	(Holy Family, Drogheda)
	WELTERWEIGHT			
(St Joseph's, Wexford)	Billy Walsh	*beat*	Joe Lowe	(Holy Trinity)
	LIGHT-MIDDLEWEIGHT			
(Sunnyside, Cork)	Kieran Joyce	*beat*	Paul McCullough	(Immaculata)
	MIDDLEWEIGHT			
(Ledley Hall, Belfast)	Ray Close	*beat*	Henry Byrne	(Sarsfield, Limerick)
	LIGHT-HEAVYWEIGHT			
(St Patrick's, Enniscorthy)	Jim O'Sullivan	*beat*	Dan Curran	(CIE)
	HEAVYWEIGHT			
(Donore, Dublin)	Joe Egan	*beat*	Liam Mervyn	(Immaculata)
	SUPER-HEAVYWEIGHT			
(Errigal)	Seán McLoughlin	*beat*	John Magee	(Tramore)

NUMBER NINE FOR O'SULLIVAN – NATIONAL SENIOR FINALS 1989

Jim O'Sullivan guaranteed himself a place in amateur boxing history when he became only the third fighter to capture a ninth Irish senior title. His unanimous victory over Ballinrobe's Peter Forde in the light-heavyweight final brought him level with Gearóid Ó Colmáin and Harry Perry. Afterwards, O'Sullivan pledged he would attempt to win a record-breaking tenth title in 1990. 'It's getting a lot easier, but I will have to try for the record now,' he said. Joe Lawlor retained his flyweight title with a 4-1 victory over Paul Buttimer. It was an all-action contest with Lawlor's superior jabbing being the decisive factor. Joe Lowe repeated his Ulster final victory over Jim Webb in the welterweight decider. Lowe did most of the attacking and deserved his unanimous victory. Denis Galvin of Moate recorded a comprehensive win over Ger Lawlor in the middleweight final. It was a superb performance by the Westmeath man as his range of punches and speed of delivery left Lawlor bewildered.

		LIGHT-FLYWEIGHT		
(St Munchin's, Limerick)	P.J. O'Halloran	*beat*	Chris Notarantonio	(Newhill, Belfast)
		FLYWEIGHT		
(Darndale)	Joe Lawlor	*beat*	Paul Buttimer	(Sunnyside, Cork)
		BANTAMWEIGHT		
(Ring, Derry)	Roy Nash	*beat*	Paul Ireland	(St George's/ St Malachy's, Belfast)
		FEATHERWEIGHT		
(CBS, Wexford)	Eddie Bolger	*beat*	Seán Deeds	(Oliver Plunkett, Belfast)
		LIGHTWEIGHT		
(Holy Trinity)	John Erskine	*beat*	Charlie Brown	(Holy Trinity)
		LIGHT-WELTERWEIGHT		
(Holy Trinity)	Eddie Fisher	*beat*	Sylvie Furlong	(St Michael's, Wexford)
		WELTERWEIGHT		
(Holy Trinity)	Joe Lowe	*beat*	Jim Webb	(Oliver Plunkett, Belfast)
		LIGHT-MIDDLEWEIGHT		
(St Joseph's, Wexford)	Billy Walsh	*beat*	Paul McCullagh	(Immaculata, Belfast)
		MIDDLEWEIGHT		
(Moate)	Denis Galvin	*beat*	Ger Lawlor	(Paulstown & Garda)
		LIGHT-HEAVYWEIGHT		
(St Patrick's, Enniscorthy)	Jim O'Sullivan	*beat*	Peter Forde	(Ballinrobe)
		HEAVYWEIGHT		
(Donore, Dublin)	Joe Egan	*beat*	Seán O'Regan	(Rylane, Cork)
		SUPER-HEAVYWEIGHT		
(Holy Family)	Paul Douglas	*beat*	Frank Curran	(St Luke's)

GRITTY DAVE 'BOY' TAKES THE IBF CROWN WITH ASSURED DISPLAY

Pound for pound it is argued that Dave 'Boy' McAuley was perhaps Ireland's greatest boxer. He came to prominence in the professional game after Barry McGuigan lost his world title in Las Vegas to Steve Cruz in 1986. Within ten months, Belfast's King's Hall witnessed a fantastic battle for the WBA flyweight title when McAuley went toe to toe with champion Fidel Bassa, only losing through sheer exhaustion in the thirteenth round. That fight was the last-ever fifteen-round world-title bout and is still considered one of the greatest to grace an Irish ring. A year later McAuley lost in the rematch to Bassa. However, on 7 June 1989 the Larne man took his place among the Irish greats with an excellent display in beating champion Duke McKenzie at the Wembley Arena to claim the IBF world flyweight title. McAuley, who had been a 5/1 outsider with the bookmakers to win that evening, boxed with power and accuracy from start to finish. Prior to the fight, McAuley told the press, 'I have the heart of a lion, and now I have a chance.' It was a statement of intent that was proved correct. Larne's greatest gloveman would go on to make six defences of his title but relinquished it after a disputed decision in Spain to Colombian Rodolfo Blanco.

LORD LONSDALE'S BELT

The Lonsdale Belt, named after Hugh Cecil Lowther, 5th Earl of Lonsdale, is one of the oldest championship belts in boxing and its origins can be traced back to London in 1909. The belt is named after Lord Lonsdale, who was patron of the National Sporting Club in Mayfair. Lonsdale was a keen boxing fan who supported the sport for many years. The belt, which is made from porcelain and gold, was presented to the champion in each British weight division. A boxer could retain the belt outright if he defended it successfully on three occasions. There are four Lonsdale Belt holders in Ireland – Freddie Gilroy, Hugh Russell, Sam Storey and Neil Sinclair. It is the ultimate prize in professional boxing on the British Isles and, until the late 1960s, outright holders were entitled to a pension of £1 a week.

GERRY STOREY (b. 1936) –
LEGENDARY TRAINER OF CHAMPIONS

Gerry Storey's dedication to boxing was rewarded in 2007 on the international stage when he received the 'Sport for Good' award at the Laureus Awards in Estoril, Portugal. During a proud career, the Holy Family trainer coached four Irish Olympic boxing squads and kept boxing thriving in Belfast during the darkest days of the Troubles. Perhaps Storey's most remarkable achievement came in the 1970s, when he was invited into the Maze Prison by both Loyalist and Republican prisoners to provide boxing lessons. His contribution to boxing and Irish sport has been immense. In addition, his son Sam is the holder of a Lonsdale Belt. In fact, three of Ireland's four Lonsdale Belt winners have represented Storey's Holy Family gym. It is a proud record for Storey and his club.

9

THE 1990s

O'SULLIVAN BREAKS RECORD – NATIONAL SENIOR FINALS 1990

The National Stadium gave a standing ovation to Enniscorthy's Jim O'Sullivan as he claimed his tenth national championship by beating Liam Mervyn in the heavyweight final on Friday 23 March. In a somewhat subdued fight, the Wexford man did enough in the opening two rounds to see off the spirited Belfast boxer and clinch an emotional achievement. Ulster boxers dominated the opening bouts of the bill with Tommy Waite, Wayne McCullough, Johnston Todd, Roy Nash and Joe Erskine all bringing titles back north. That dominance was broken by Michael Carruth in the light-welterweight final, when he beat Billy Boyd of the Holy Family club. Johnston Todd, who beat Joe Lawlor in the bantamweight final, was one of the most talented boxers to have come out of the County Antrim town of Ballyclare. Johnston died suddenly in November 2011, aged 43. He was noted for his electrifying punching power and claimed a bronze at light-flyweight at the 1986 Commonwealth Games. At his funeral, former Ulster IABA president Pat McCrory said, 'Everyone in boxing will miss Johnston, he was a great lad, and boy could he punch!'

	LIGHT-FLYWEIGHT			
(Cairn Lodge, Belfast)	Tommy Waite	*beat*	Donal Hosford	(Cork)
	FLYWEIGHT			
(Albert Foundry)	Wayne McCullough	*beat*	Martin McQuillan	(Drogheda)
	BANTAMWEIGHT			
(Holy Family)	Johnston Todd	*beat*	Joe Lawlor	(Darndale)
	FEATHERWEIGHT			
(Ring, Derry)	Roy Nash	*beat*	Paul Griffin	(Drimnagh)

	LIGHTWEIGHT			
(Holy Trinity)	John Erskine	*beat*	John McEvoy	(Edenmore, Dublin)
	LIGHT-WELTERWEIGHT			
(Drimnagh)	Michael Carruth	*beat*	Billy Boyd	(Holy Family)
	WELTERWEIGHT			
(Holy Trinity)	Eddie Fisher	*beat*	Eamonn Magee	(Sacred Heart, Belfast)
	LIGHT-MIDDLEWEIGHT			
(Enniscorthy)	Billy Walsh	*beat*	Gordon Joyce	(Sunnyside, Cork)
	MIDDLEWEIGHT			
(Moate)	Denis Galvin	*beat*	Martin Brennan	(Westport)
	LIGHT-HEAVYWEIGHT			
(Rathfriland, Down)	Paul McKay	*beat*	Dan Curran	(CIE)
	HEAVYWEIGHT			
(St Patrick's, Wexford)	Jim O'Sullivan	*beat*	Lee Mervyn	(Immaculata)
	SUPER-HEAVYWEIGHT			
(Holy Family)	Paul Douglas	*beat*	George Douglas	(South Meath)

WAYNE WITHDRAWS, JOE CLAIMS TITLE – NATIONAL SENIOR FINALS 1991

The eagerly awaited bantamweight final between Joe Lawlor and Wayne McCullough was cancelled at the last minute as McCullough was forced to withdraw due to chickenpox. In the welterweight final there was also a walkover for Billy Walsh after Eddie Fisher withdrew due to a hand injury. Professional stars Barry McGuigan and Stephen Collins were among the near-capacity audience and, as a former world featherweight champion, McGuigan enjoyed the fight between Roy Nash and Paul Griffin. It ended in triumph for Dubliner Griffin, who won a unanimous decision against the defending champion. Griffin deserved his success, although it was much closer than expected. He started extremely well and while Nash recovered in the second round, the Dubliner did enough in the final session to grab victory.

Another Dubliner, Brian Geraghty, was not as lucky as he went down to a 4-1 defeat by Waterford's Neil Gough. Gough took a standing count in the opening round of the light-welterweight final but recovered well and his sharper, neater punching swayed the decision his way. The light-middleweight final was a close affair with Belfast's Joe Lowe scraping through on a 3-2 verdict.

	LIGHT-FLYWEIGHT	
(Cavan)	Paul Cosgrove	*walkover*

	FLYWEIGHT			
(Sunnyside, Cork)	Paul Buttimer	beat	P.J. O'Halloran	(St Munchin's, Limerick)

	BANTAMWEIGHT	
(Darndale, Dublin)	Joe Lawlor	*walkover*

	FEATHERWEIGHT			
(Drimnagh, Dublin)	Paul Griffin	beat	Roy Nash	(Ring, Derry)

	LIGHTWEIGHT			
(St George's, Belfast)	Paul Ireland	beat	Seamus McCann	(Holy Family)

	LIGHT-WELTERWEIGHT			
(Waterford)	Neil Gough	beat	Brian Geraghty	(Mount Tallant)

	WELTERWEIGHT	
(Wexford)	Billy Walsh	*walkover*

	LIGHT-MIDDLEWEIGHT			
(Holy Trinity)	Joe Lowe	beat	Gordon Joyce	(Sunnyside, Cork)

	MIDDLEWEIGHT			
(Moate)	Denis Galvin	beat	Chris Cullen	(Clonoe, Tyrone)

	LIGHT-HEAVYWEIGHT			
(Ledley Hall, Belfast)	Mark Delaney	beat	Ger Lawlor	(Paulstown)

	HEAVYWEIGHT			
(Avona, Dublin)	Ray Kane	beat	Peter Forde	(Castlebar)

	SUPER-HEAVYWEIGHT			
(South Meath)	George Douglas	beat	Seán Murphy	(St Michael's, Wexford)

CARRUTH VICTORY ENDS IN UPROAR

Despite winning his Irish senior quarterfinal against Edenderry's Martin McBride in an emphatic fashion, Michael Carruth's win was not well received by his opponent. The welterweight fight, which took place on 9 January 1992, was awarded to Carruth on a convincing 23-3 verdict. McBride, however, was incensed and refused to shake his opponent's hand as a missile landed in the ring, catching Carruth on the leg. McBride then proceeded to sit in the middle of the ring for a full five minutes until the secretary of the IABA, Art O'Brien, pleaded with the boxer to leave as catcalls and slow-hand claps resounded around the arena. Eventually, McBride left the ring and gardaí were called to investigate the missile-throwing incident. Boxing officials were incensed by the events of the night.

BATTLING FOR BARCELONA – NATIONAL SENIOR FINALS 1992

The Irish senior finals on Friday 17 January 1992 pitted Michael Carruth against his great friend Billy Walsh for what was seen to be a battle for a place on the Irish team for the Barcelona Olympic Games. Their welterweight final saw Walsh going for his eighth national title against Carruth, a three-time former champion from the Drimnagh club. The fight had everything and the packed house rose as one after a thrilling contest, which Carruth won by 12-9. In the earlier bouts, both Wayne McCullough and Paul Griffin put in superb displays when taking the bantamweight and featherweight crowns respectively. McCullough, who had missed the 1991 championships due to chickenpox, impressed as he beat the reigning champion Joe Lawlor 33-19 while European champion Griffin exhibited all his skills in his victory over Chris Notarantonio of Belfast.

	LIGHT-FLYWEIGHT			
(Drogheda)	Martin McQuillan	beat	P.J. O'Halloran	(St Munchin's, Limerick)
	FLYWEIGHT			
(Sunnyside, Cork)	Paul Buttimer	beat	Damaen Kelly	(Holy Trinity)
	BANTAMWEIGHT			
(Albert Foundry)	Wayne McCullough	beat	Joe Lawlor	(Darndale)
	FEATHERWEIGHT			
(Drimnagh)	Paul Griffin	beat	Chris Notarantonio	(Newhill, Belfast)
	LIGHTWEIGHT			
(Antrim)	Mark Winters	beat	Paul Ireland	(St George's, Belfast)
	LIGHT-WELTERWEIGHT			
(Sacred Heart, Belfast)	Eamonn Magee	beat	Neil Gough	(Waterford)
	WELTERWEIGHT			
(Drimnagh, Dublin)	Michael Carruth	beat	Billy Walsh	(St Ibar's, Wexford)
	LIGHT-MIDDLEWEIGHT			
(Holy Trinity)	Joe Lowe	beat	Gordon Joyce	(Sunnyside, Cork)
	MIDDLEWEIGHT			
(Moate)	Denis Galvin	beat	Hugh Byrne	(St Munchin's, Limerick)
	LIGHT-HEAVYWEIGHT			
(Holy Trinity)	Mark Delaney	beat	Ger Lawlor	(Paulstown)
	HEAVYWEIGHT			
(St Agnes, Belfast)	Tony Currie	beat	Paul Douglas	(Holy Family)
	SUPER-HEAVYWEIGHT			
(Smithboro, Monaghan)	Kevin McBride	beat	Colin Robinson	(Antrim)

THE FAIRY TALE THAT ENDED IN COURT – EASTWOOD *v.* MCGUIGAN

The 'father-son' relationship between Barney Eastwood and Barry McGuigan in the 1980s has been well documented. Such was the respect with which McGuigan regarded his manager that the phrase 'Thank you, Mr Eastwood' was the subject of a comedy song by Dermot Morgan in 1986. In February 1981, millionaire bookmaker and promoter Eastwood believed that he could make McGuigan a world champion and signed the Clones Cyclone. That hunch became a reality in Queen's Park Rangers's Loftus Road ground in June 1985 in front of 27,000 fans when McGuigan dethroned Panama's Eusebio Pedrosa to take the WBA featherweight title. 'I love this man,' Barry had told the watching millions as he embraced Eastwood in the ring that night. A year later in Las Vegas, the relationship between the manager and the fighter began to disintegrate as Texan Steve Cruz took McGuigan's title in the searing heat of the Nevada desert. In 1987, Eastwood released McGuigan from his contract, but the bitterness over money and earnings festered and ended up in court.

That court appearance was merely a curtain-raiser to a further Belfast case involving the two men, which had the Irish and British public enthralled for over a month in 1992. The trouble began when McGuigan appeared in a video entitled 'The Barry McGuigan Story' in 1988, in which McGuigan made claims about Eastwood which incensed him, and which led the boxer's former manager to bring proceedings for defamation. The case opened in early February and lasted twenty-three days. It was nasty, to say the least. Eastwood was labelled a 'liar' in court by McGuigan's team, while McGuigan was portrayed as a boxer who was as 'green as grass' and who had turned against the man who had brought him to a world title. Thousands of pounds were spent bringing expert witnesses to Belfast. When the jury returned its decision on 9 March, it was McGuigan who came off worse – considerably worse. The jury found in Eastwood's favour. The legal bill was thought to be in the region of £750,000.

It was a bitter end to a bloody battle. Years later, Barney's son Stephen put the relationship in context. 'As a member of the Eastwood family I can candidly state my father ate, drank and slept the Barry McGuigan project from the moment he signed up the fighter,' said Stephen. 'My brothers agree with me that McGuigan for a time was Dad's favourite son. It was as simple as that in those early days, but when people got between that arrangement it soon began to sour,' he added.

OLYMPIC TRIALS MEET WITH PROTESTS

In the aftermath of the 1992 finals, the IABA ordered that five boxing trials would be held for the right to represent Ireland at the Barcelona Olympic Games. This unusual move was greeted with protests from the reigning champions who, given the close margin of their victories in the finals, were re-matched with the runners-up at the Ringside Club on 14 February. Should the reigning champions lose their bouts, a final box-off would take place the following day. However, two reigning champions, light-welterweight Eamon Magee and heavyweight Tony Currie, refused to partake in the bouts, which meant that Neil Gough and Paul Douglas were chosen by default to represent Ireland in the Barcelona qualifying events. In the end, all three champions – Paul Buttimer, Michael Carruth and John Lowe – were victorious. Buttimer was tested by Damaen Kelly and took the fight on a 20-18 margin, while Carruth comfortably beat Billy Walsh, who announced his retirement after the fight. Most emphatic of the winners was Joe Lowey who stopped Cork's Gordon Joyce in the first round of their bout.

MICHAEL CARRUTH – THE HISTORY MAKER

On 8 August 1992, Michael Carruth made Irish sporting history when he claimed the gold medal at the Barcelona Olympics in the welterweight class. The clash with Cuba's Juan Hernández Sierra was watched by millions of fans in Ireland and Michael's victory prompted wild scenes of celebration. Carruth's gold medal came shortly after teammate Wayne McCullough had to settle for the silver in the bantamweight final. It was the first Olympic gold medal for Ireland since Ronnie Delaney had won the Men's 1,500 metres at the 1956 Olympic Games in Melbourne. Famously, prior to his final, Carruth told his father Austin, who was in his corner as Irish coach, that 'Ronnie Delany's time is up', such was his confidence. RTÉ carried live coverage of the Carruth family's reaction in their home in Dublin as the fight progressed. Fred Tiedt, Ireland's silver medallist at the Melbourne Olympic Games, sat with the family to witness the historic moment.

WAYNE MCCULLOUGH – THE POCKET ROCKET

Of all the decorated boxers to come from this island, Wayne McCullough's record is second to none. His achievement in winning a world title in Japan alone was monumental in boxing terms and a true reflection of his undoubted ability and class. Add to that a silver medal at Olympic level, together with gold at the Commonwealth Games, and it is evident that Wayne McCullough's pedigree was top class. McCullough was born in Belfast's Percy Street in July 1970. His ability as an amateur came to the fore during his time as a young boxer in the Albert Foundry club on Belfast's West Circular Road. By the mid-1980s, with a plethora of Ulster and Irish titles under his belt, he had become one of the most formidable exponents of the art in Ireland. He represented Ireland in the flyweight division at the Olympic Games in Seoul in 1988, where he famously carried the tricolour. In 1990, McCullough won a gold medal at the Commonwealth Games in Auckland, New Zealand, again in the flyweight division. However, it was at the Barcelona Olympics in 1992 that was to see the Pocket Rocket's greatest amateur triumph when he claimed silver in the bantamweight class, losing to the experienced Cuban Joel Casamayor.

He turned professional in 1993, having enjoyed an amateur record of 319 fights, winning all but eleven, with over 100 wins by knockout. Wayne moved to Las Vegas to train under Eddie Futch, who agreed to look after him, having seeing him box at the Olympics. Within a year of turning pro, he had won the North American Boxing Federation title. On 30 July 1995, less than two and a half years after his paid debut, he won the WBC championship by beating the champion Yasuei Yakushiji in Nagoya, Japan, to become Ireland's first WBC bantamweight world champion. He was the first (and only) Irish or British fighter to travel to Japan and win a belt. McCullough defended his title twice before vacating the belt and moving up in weight to challenge WBC super-bantamweight champion Daniel Zaragoza, but he lost due to a split decision after what was considered the 1997 'Fight of the Year' by *The Ring* magazine.

BOXING IN THE WAKE OF TRAGEDY

A mere six days after the Shankill Road bombing in Belfast, Ireland faced England at the National Stadium in an eagerly anticipated international. One of the stars that night was bantamweight Tommy Waite of the Cairn Lodge ABC, who had been close by when the bomb exploded in Frizzell's shop, killing ten people in what was one of the most shocking outrages of the Troubles. With the international balanced finely at two bouts each, Waite, a Shankill Road man, was given a fine reception by the crowd as he prepared to face Gary Licette of Torbay. After a psychologically testing week, during which he had attended the funerals of many victims of the bombing, Waite boxed his way to a fine victory on a 9-8 margin.

Waite admitted afterwards, 'Naturally enough I was very upset by what happened, and with funerals every day of the week, and I suppose I was not completely tuned in for the fight.' Waite's victory was to inspire Ireland to a 6-3 win over England, with Darren Corbett knocking out ABA champion Michael McKenzie with a thunderous punch in the first round of their heavyweight bout. Apart from Waite and Corbett, Ireland's winners on the night were Denis Galvin, Patrick Deane, Neil Gough and Danny Ryan. It had been an emotional night during which sport prevailed after a week of death and tears on the streets of Belfast and beyond. As a professional, Tommy Waite would go on to claim the Irish bantamweight title in 1997 and the British title with a fourth-round stoppage of Ady Lewis in September 2000.

CARRUTH AND McCULLOUGH REST-UP: NATIONAL SENIOR FINALS 1993

The success of Ireland's Olympic squad in 1992 saw interest in the 1993 finals at a fever pitch with over 500 patrons unable to gain admission to the National Stadium. Both Wayne McCullough and Michael Carruth had decided to take a break from the championships and the bantamweight and welterweight crowns went to Munster clubs. Paul Buttimer of the Sunnyside Club in Cork beat Belfast's Tommy Waite to claim McCullough's title, while Waterford's Neil Gough's ring craft saw him beat Eddie Fisher of the Holy Trinity club. It was fitting that another Waterford man, Peter Crotty, was inducted into the IABA's Hall of Fame on the night. He was afforded a rapturous reception as he was presented the award by Carruth and McCullough. Seven of the titles went to Ulster clubs, with Paul Griffin and Mark Sutton the only winners from Dublin clubs.

		LIGHT-FLYWEIGHT		
(Holy Family, Drogheda)	Martin McQuillan	*beat*	Jim Prior	(Darndale, Dublin)
		FLYWEIGHT		
(Holy Trinity)	Damaen Kelly	*beat*	Donal Hosford	(Greenmount, Cork)
		BANTAMWEIGHT		
(Sunnyside, Cork)	Paul Buttimer	*beat*	Tommy Waite	(Cairn Lodge, Belfast)
		FEATHERWEIGHT		
(Mount Tallant)	Paul Griffin	*beat*	Paul Ireland	(St George's/ St Malachy's, Belfast)
		LIGHTWEIGHT		
(Antrim)	Mark Winters	*beat*	Glen Stephens	(Drimnagh, Dublin)
		LIGHT-WELTERWEIGHT		
(Sacred Heart, Belfast)	Eamonn Magee	*beat*	Billy Walsh	(St Colman's, Cork)
		WELTERWEIGHT		
(St Paul's, Waterford)	Neil Gough	*beat*	Eddie Fisher	(Holy Trinity, Belfast)
		LIGHT-MIDDLEWEIGHT		
(Holy Trinity)	Jim Webb	*beat*	Anthony McFadden	(Dunfanaghy)
		MIDDLEWEIGHT		

(Raphoe, Donegal)	Danny Ryan	*beat*	Denis Galvin	(Moate)

LIGHT-HEAVYWEIGHT

(St Saviour's, Dublin)	Mark Sutton	*beat*	Mark Delaney	(Holy Trinity, Belfast)

HEAVYWEIGHT

(Holy Family)	Paul Douglas	*beat*	Dan Curran	(CIE, Dublin)

SUPER-HEAVYWEIGHT

(Holy Family)	Darren Corbett	*beat*	George Douglas	(South Meath)

GORDON JOYCE BOUNCES BACK – NATIONAL SENIOR FINALS 1994

Paul Griffin, the 1991 European amateur featherweight champion who had been pushed to the limit to beat Paul Ireland in 1993, was assured in beating Ireland and claiming his fourth successive national featherweight title. Griffin was in total control, catching Ireland with perfectly delivered right and left counters. Denis Galvin avenged his 1993 loss to Donegal's Danny Ryan with a 9-8 win after an explosive fight. Galvin, boxing out of St Saviour's club in Dublin, staggered Ryan with a left in the opening round but the Donegal man scored with thumping right hands and the verdict was in doubt until the last seconds. Another former champion, Gordon Joyce, claimed his first title since 1988 when he won the light-heavyweight crown with a competent victory over Adrian Sheerin of Swinford.

LIGHT-FLYWEIGHT

(Holy Family, Drogheda)	Martin McQuillan	*beat*	Jim Prior	(Darndale)

FLYWEIGHT

(Holy Trinity)	Damaen Kelly	*beat*	Donal Hosford	(Greenmount, Cork)

BANTAMWEIGHT

(Cairn Lodge, Belfast)	Tommy Waite	*beat*	Danny McAree	(Immaculata)

FEATHERWEIGHT

(Mount Tallant)	Paul Griffin	*beat*	Paul Ireland	(St George's)

LIGHTWEIGHT

(Crumlin, Dublin)	Glen Stephens	*beat*	Eddie Bolger	(CBS, Wexford)

LIGHT-WELTERWEIGHT

(St Colman's, Cork)	Billy Walsh	*beat*	Seán Barrett	(Rylane, Cork)

WELTERWEIGHT

(St Paul's, Waterford)	Neil Gough	*beat*	Neil Sinclair	(Holy Family)

LIGHT-MIDDLEWEIGHT

(Holy Trinity)	Jim Webb	*beat*	Anthony McFadden	(Dunfanaghy)

MIDDLEWEIGHT

(Moate)	Denis Galvin	*beat*	Danny Ryan	(Raphoe)

LIGHT-HEAVYWEIGHT

(Sunnyside, Cork)	Gordon Joyce	*beat*	Adrian Sheerin	(Swinford)

	HEAVYWEIGHT			
(Holy Family)	Paul Douglas	*beat*	Pat Doran	(Phibsboro)

	SUPER-HEAVYWEIGHT		
(South Meath)	George Douglas	*walkover*	

'SINKY' SHOWS HIS CLASS – NATIONAL SENIOR FINALS 1995

Neil Sinclair, a Commonwealth Games welterweight gold medallist, deposed of Neil Gough in a superb repeat of the 1994 final. The Belfast boxer put Gough on the canvas as he enjoyed a 15-9 win that was never in doubt. Within weeks, Sinclair was to turn professional under Barry Hearn. On a night when Ulster boxers did well, Commonwealth silver medallist Martin Reneghan lost the lightweight decider to defending champion Glen Stephens from Dublin, whose superb tactics thwarted the Ulster boxer. Damaen Kelly clinched a hat-trick of titles with an impressive 16-5 win over Dubliner Brendan Walsh, while Paul Douglas regained the super-heavyweight title when he outpointed defending champion George Douglas 13-8. It was Douglas's fifth title at heavyweight and super-heavyweight.

	LIGHT-FLYWEIGHT			
(Darndale)	Jim Prior	*beat*	Colin Moffatt	(Holy Family)
	FLYWEIGHT			
(Holy Trinity)	Damaen Kelly	*beat*	Brendan Walsh	(Darndale)
	BANTAMWEIGHT			
(St Saviour's)	Willie Valentine	*beat*	Donal Hosford	(Cork)
	FEATHERWEIGHT			
(Newry)	Adrian Patterson	*beat*	Terry Carlyle	(Sacred Heart, Dublin)
	LIGHTWEIGHT			
(Crumlin)	Glen Stephens	*beat*	Martin Reneghan	(Keady)
	LIGHT-WELTERWEIGHT			
(Lurgan)	Glen McClarnon	*beat*	Billy Walsh	(St Colman's, Cork)
	WELTERWEIGHT			
(Holy Family)	Neil Sinclair	*beat*	Neil Gough	(Waterford)
	LIGHT-MIDDLEWEIGHT			
(Fermoy)	Declan Higgins	*beat*	Michael Roche	(Sunnyside)
	MIDDLEWEIGHT			
(Holy Trinity)	Brian Magee	*beat*	Denis Galvin	(St Saviour's, Dublin)
	LIGHT-HEAVYWEIGHT			
(Cairn Lodge, Belfast)	Stephen Kirk	*beat*	Gordon Joyce	(Sunnyside, Cork)
	HEAVYWEIGHT			
(Kilfenora, Clare)	James Clancy	*beat*	Mark Sutton	(St Saviour's, Dublin)
	SUPER-HEAVYWEIGHT			
(Holy Family)	Paul Douglas	*beat*	George Douglas	(South Meath)

COLLINS WINS THE PSYCHOLOGICAL BATTLE WITH EUBANK

Confusion was the order of the day on 6 February 1995, when Chris Eubank arrived at Jury's Hotel in Dublin to publicise his forthcoming fight with Steve Collins. Eubank, well known for his brashness and flamboyant dress code, was upstaged at the event when Collins arrived dressed in Victorian tweeds, accompanied by an Irish wolfhound whose presence was not welcomed by the hotel's security guards. All was amicable until Collins accused Eubank of betraying his African roots in portraying himself as an aristocratic Englishman. Later, in the hotel lift, the Lord Mayor of Dublin, John Gormley, happened to suggest that it was a 'pity' that Eubank would not be able to take in all of the sites of Dublin. 'F**k the city,' responded Eubank. 'I have had enough of your niceties, I am here to box.' The Lord Mayor was less than impressed and a motion was passed unanimously by the Dublin City Council later that evening, calling on Eubank to apologise. Two days later, wise heads prevailed and Eubank did indeed apologise to the Lord Mayor for 'losing his head'.

The fight itself between Eubank and Collins took place in Mill Street Arena, Cork, on 18 March. Psychology was to the fore on that memorable night as Collins had let it be known that he had been 'hypnotised' before the fight. As Eubank strutted to the ring, Collins sat with his earphones in, seemingly oblivious to his opponent. In rounds eight and ten, Collins put Eubank to the canvas as he went on to win over twelve rounds and relieve Eubank of his WBO super-middleweight title

STEVE COLLINS – THE CELTIC WARRIOR

Steve Collins, nicknamed the Celtic Warrior, was born in Dublin on 21 July 1964. He came from a well-known boxing family (his uncle was former Irish champion Jack O'Rourke) and was considered one of the toughest fighters of recent times – and one of the most popular of the late 1990s. He was never stopped in a high-profile career and once joked that his chin was sponsored by Readymix Concrete. In 1994, he defeated Chris Pyatt to secure the WBO middleweight belt. The following year he relinquished this title, moved up to super-middleweight and defeated Chris Eubank in Millstreet, Cork, to win the WBO title. He defended this title successfully seven times, including a second meeting with Eubank and two victories over Nigel Benn.

FRANCIS BARRATT MAKES HISTORY – NATIONAL SENIOR FINALS 1996

Francis Barrett made history when he became the first member of Ireland's Travelling community to win an Irish senior title. The 19-year-old from Galway beat Cork's John Morrissey in the light-welterweight decider. Winner of five underage Irish titles, Barrett wrapped up his win in the last round when he pressed Morrissey and scored with solid punches to the head and body. At flyweight, Damaen Kelly, who was recovering from a hand operation, dominated Dubliner David Sweetman as he surged to a 21-3 success. Jimmy Prior, the Dublin light-flyweight, retained his title with a 16-6 win over the Ulster champion Colin Moffatt from Bangor.

	LIGHT-FLYWEIGHT			
(Darndale)	Jim Prior	*beat*	Colin Moffatt	(Holy Family)
	FLYWEIGHT			
(Holy Trinity)	Damaen Kelly	*beat*	Donal Sweetman	(Dublin)
	BANTAMWEIGHT			
(Drogheda)	Damian McKenna	*beat*	Oliver Duddy	(Coleraine)
	FEATHERWEIGHT			
(Newry)	Adrian Patterson	*beat*	Terry Carlyle	(Sacred Heart, Dublin)
	LIGHTWEIGHT			
(Keady)	Martin Reneghan	*beat*	Owen Montague	(Antrim)
	LIGHT-WELTERWEIGHT			
(Galway)	Francis Barrett	*beat*	John Morrissey	(Sunnyside, Cork)
	WELTERWEIGHT			
(Waterford)	Neil Gough	*beat*	Seanie Barrett	(Rylane, Cork)
	LIGHT-MIDDLEWEIGHT			
(Fermoy)	Declan Higgins	*beat*	John Kelly	(Manorhamilton)
	MIDDLEWEIGHT			
(Holy Trinity)	Brian Magee	*beat*	Brian Crowley	(Ennis)
	LIGHT-HEAVYWEIGHT			
(Cairn Lodge)	Stephen Kirk	*beat*	Gordon Joyce	(Sunnyside, Cork)
	HEAVYWEIGHT			
(St Saviour's, Dublin)	Cathal O'Grady	*beat*	Paul Douglas	(Holy Family)
	SUPER-HEAVYWEIGHT			
(Wexford)	Seán Murphy	*beat*	Timmy O'Connor	(Knocknagoshel, Kerry)

IRELAND FIND THE GOING TOUGH – ATLANTA OLYMPIC GAMES 1996

Damaen Kelly and Brian Magee of Belfast's Holy Trinity club boxed their way to quarterfinals spots at the Atlanta Olympic Games but both were to lose out. Kelly had stormed his way through the flyweight division with victories over Yulian Strogov of Bulgaria in the first series. He then beat Australia's Hussein Hussein 27-20 in the second series, but lost to silver medallist Bulat Jumadilov of Kazakhstan 13-6 in his quarterfinal. Magee's progress was similar as he beat Randall Thompson of Canada 13-5 in the first series and Cameroon's Bertrand Tetsia on an 11-6 scoreline in the second series. His quarterfinal against Mohamed Bahari was a close contest but the Algerian pulled away in the last round to claim a 15-9 victory. It was disappointment for Galway's Francis Barrett who defeated Zely Fereira dos Santos of Brazil 32-7 in the first series, but found bronze medallist Fathi Missaoui of Tunisia too clever and lost 18-6. Ireland's only other competitor, heavyweight Cathal O'Grady of the St Saviour's club in Dublin, lost to Garth Da Silva of New Zealand in the first series.

ULSTER AGAIN TO THE FORE – NATIONAL SENIOR FINALS 1997

Damaen Kelly successfully made the transition from flyweight to bantamweight when he beat defending champion Damien McKenna at a packed National Stadium. Kelly, who also won the Best Boxer award, spearheaded an Ulster sweep of the lighter weights. Jim Rooney, the 19-year-old Ulster senior champion, defeated Jim Prior in a fight which was scored manually by the judges after a computer malfunction. Cork's hopes were dashed at lightweight and light-welterweight when Declan Barrett and Patrick Walsh both lost comprehensively. Brian Magee, the defending middleweight champion, outpointed the Romanian-born Corkman, Ciprian Surugiu, forcing him to take a count in the third round. At light-heavyweight, Stephen Kirk ran Kelly close for boxer of the night when he displayed all his class in defeating Aidan Sheerin of Swinford.

	LIGHT-FLYWEIGHT			
(Star, Belfast)	Jim Rooney	*beat*	Jim Prior	(Darndale)
	FLYWEIGHT			
(Saints, Belfast)	Liam Cunningham	*beat*	Donal Hosford	(Greenmount)
	BANTAMWEIGHT			
(Holy Trinity)	Damaen Kelly	*beat*	Damian McKenna	(Holy Family, Drogheda)
	FEATHERWEIGHT			
(Dockers, Belfast)	Peadar O'Donnell	*beat*	Aodh Carlyle	(Sacred Heart, Dublin)
	LIGHTWEIGHT			
(Dundalk)	Eamonn McEneaney	*beat*	Declan Barrett	(Cork)

	LIGHT-WELTERWEIGHT			
(Holy Family)	Glen McClarnon	*beat*	Patrick 'Pa' Walsh	(Cork)

	WELTERWEIGHT			
(Waterford)	Neil Gough	*beat*	Willie Cowan	(Monkstown)

	LIGHT-MIDDLEWEIGHT			
(Sunnyside, Cork)	Michael Roche	*beat*	Tom Fitzgerald	(Cork)

	MIDDLEWEIGHT			
(Holy Trinity)	Brian Magee	*beat*	Ciprian Petrea (CP) Surugio	(Crumlin)

	LIGHT-HEAVYWEIGHT			
(Cairn Lodge, Belfast)	Stephen Kirk	*beat*	Aidan Sheerin	(Mayo)

	HEAVYWEIGHT			
(Corpus Christi, Limerick)	John Kiely	*beat*	James Clancy	(Phoenix, Dublin)

	SUPER-HEAVYWEIGHT			
(St Joseph's, Sligo)	Stephen Reynolds	*beat*	Brendan Kirrane	(Limerick)

BARRETT CLAIMS BRITISH AMATEUR TITLE

Despite losing in the Irish senior semi-finals to Monkstown's Willie Cowan, Francis Barrett took the British ABA welterweight title five days later on 7 March, when he defeated Tim Smith from the Trojan club in Birmingham. In doing so, he became the first boxer from the west of Ireland to take a British amateur title. Barrett's win over Smith meant that he had completed a hat-trick of successes against the top three welterweights in England, having earlier accounted for Michael Jennings and Tony Casey. After getting married in September 1996, Barratt left Ireland for London and competed in the welterweight division. He then took the unprecedented step of boxing for the senior titles in both Britain and Ireland, two tournaments which almost overlapped. It was an awesome period for Barrett, who left after the ABA final for Memphis, where he was guest of honour for its St Patrick's Day parade.

MARY LAWLOR MAKES IRISH BOXING HISTORY

Mother of six Mary Lawlor made Irish boxing history at the National Stadium on 3 April 1998 when she became the first woman to referee a competitive bout at headquarters. The occasion was the National Youth Finals and Mary's performance received all-round acclaim. One bout she was not permitted to officiate in, however, was one in which her son, Dermot, won with a unanimous verdict over Paul Traynor of Belfast.

'BEST BOXER' FOR NEIL GOUGH – NATIONAL SENIOR FINALS 1998

Seven of the eight defending champions retained their titles, with Liam Cunningham the only fighter to lose out. Cunningham came up against a shrewd boxer in Waterford's Nigel Murphy, who created the shock of the night, throwing swift left hooks in the first and second rounds that put Cunningham on the canvas. After the second, the referee decided he had seen enough and led the 1997 champion to his corner. James Rooney, the Belfast light-flyweight, retained his crown on a walkover. New champions crowned were Adrian Sheerin, Mark Wickham and Bernard Dunne, along with Cunningham's conqueror Martin Murphy. Dunne was efficient in stopping Michael Burke from Gorey inside two rounds. Brian Magee won his fourth middleweight title when he outclassed Kevin Walsh and the Best Boxer Award went to Neil Gough. Gough took his sixth title when he retained his welterweight crown with an easier-than-expected win over Francis Barrett.

	LIGHT-FLYWEIGHT			
(Star, Belfast)	Jim Rooney *walkover*			
	FLYWEIGHT			
(Waterford)	Nigel Murphy	*beat*	Liam Cunningham	(Saints, Belfast)
	BANTAMWEIGHT			
(CIE)	Bernard Dunne	*beat*	Michael Burke	(Gorey)
	FEATHERWEIGHT			
(Dockers, Belfast)	Peadar O'Donnell	*beat*	Terry Carlyle	(Sacred Heart, Dublin)
	LIGHTWEIGHT			
(Dundalk)	Eamonn McEneaney	*beat*	Aodh Carlyle	(Sacred Heart, Dublin)
	LIGHT-WELTERWEIGHT			
(Enniscorthy)	Mark Wickham	*beat*	Paul McCloskey	(Dungiven)
	WELTERWEIGHT			
(St Paul's, Waterford)	Neil Gough	*beat*	Francis Barrett	(Galway)
	LIGHT-MIDDLEWEIGHT			
(Sunnyside, Cork)	Michael Roche	*beat*	Tom Fitzgerald	(Cork)
	MIDDLEWEIGHT			
(Holy Trinity)	Brian Magee	*beat*	Kevin Walsh	(St Colman's, Cork)
	LIGHT-HEAVYWEIGHT			
(Swinford, Mayo)	Adrian Sheerin	*beat*	Alo Kelly	(Brosna, Offaly)
	HEAVYWEIGHT			
(Corpus Christi, Limerick)	John Kiely	*beat*	Ben McGarrigle	(Omagh)
	SUPER-HEAVYWEIGHT			
(St Joseph's, Sligo)	Stephen Reynolds	*beat*	John Kinsella	(Crumlin, Dublin)

BROTHERS' MIXED RESULTS –
NATIONAL SENIOR FINALS 1999

The long road to the Sydney Olympic Games began for Ireland's boxers at the 1999 senior finals. Bernard Dunne found himself in a bruising featherweight final with Terry Carlyle, which ended at 7-7, before the countback gave Dunne a single point victory by 44-43. There was compensation for the Carlyle family when Aodh, Terry's brother, recorded a 13-5 victory over Louth's Eugene McEneaney of the Dealgan club. Liam Cunningham from Belfast was superb in the closing stages of his bout against Darren Campbell of the Glin Club in Dublin and ran out a clear winner by eight points. Alas, there was to be no family double as Harry Cunningham lost out to 20-year-old James Rooney of the Star ABC in Belfast. Louth did claim a title when bantamweight Damien McKenna from Drogheda beat Billy Waite of the Holy Family on an assured 6-0 scoreline. The Reynolds bothers, Alan and Stephen, took both the light-heavyweight and heavyweight titles back to Sligo, while Michael Roche of Cork's Sunnyside claimed his third successive light-middleweight crown with a 9-5 win over Drimnagh's Frank O'Brien.

	LIGHT-FLYWEIGHT			
(Star, Belfast)	Jim Rooney	*beat*	Harry Cunningham	(Saints, Belfast)
	FLYWEIGHT			
(Saints, Belfast)	Liam Cunningham	*beat*	Darren Campbell	(Glin)
	BANTAMWEIGHT			
(Drogheda)	Damien McKenna	*beat*	Billy Waite	(Holy Family)
	FEATHERWEIGHT			
(CIE)	Bernard Dunne	*beat*	Terry Carlyle	(Sacred Heart, Dublin)
	LIGHTWEIGHT			
(Sacred Heart, Dublin)	Aodh Carlyle	*beat*	Eamonn McEneaney	(Dundalk)
	LIGHT-WELTERWEIGHT			
(Rylane, Cork)	Seán Barrett	*beat*	Francis Barrett	(Galway)
	WELTERWEIGHT			
(St Paul's, Waterford)	Neil Gough	*beat*	Kevin Cumiskey	(Tralee)
	LIGHT-MIDDLEWEIGHT			
(Sunnyside, Cork)	Michael Roche	*beat*	Frankie O'Brien	(Drimnagh)
	MIDDLEWEIGHT			
(Holy Trinity)	Conal Carmichael	*beat*	Ian Timms	(CIE)
	LIGHT-HEAVYWEIGHT			
(Sligo)	Alan Reynolds	*beat*	Tommy Sheehan	(Athy)
	HEAVYWEIGHT			
(Sligo)	Stephen Reynolds	*beat*	John Kiely	(Corpus Christi, Limerick)
	SUPER-HEAVYWEIGHT			
(Crumlin)	John Kinsella	*beat*	Jason McDonagh	(Westport)

10

THE TWENTY-FIRST CENTURY

TWO FAMILY DOUBLES AT THE STADIUM – NATIONAL SENIOR FINALS 2000

Dungiven southpaw Paul McCloskey struggled to find his rhythm against the supremely fit Seán Barratt in the light-welterweight final. Barrett, a cross-country and marathon runner, led narrowly after an action-packed first round. He then opened a three-point lead, forcing McCloskey onto the back foot with superb counter-punching. Still trailing going into the last round, McCloskey scored with neat hooks but finished up one point behind his rival at the finish. Waterford's Neil Gough claimed his eighth senior title in the welterweight final, while Belfast brothers Harry and Liam Cunningham scored a quick family double in the light-flyweight and flyweight divisions. The Cunninghams' feat was matched by Sligo brothers Alan and Stephen Reynolds, who completed a second family double, taking the light-heavyweight and heavyweight crowns respectively.

	LIGHT-FLYWEIGHT			
(Saints, Belfast)	Harry Cunningham	beat	John Paul Kinsella	(Ballybrack)
	FLYWEIGHT			
(Saints, Belfast)	Liam Cunningham	beat	Damian Campbell	(Glin)
	BANTAMWEIGHT			
(Drogheda)	Damien McKenna	beat	Michael Burke	(St Ibar's)
	FEATHERWEIGHT			
(CIE)	Bernard Dunne	beat	James Phillips	(St Michael's, Athy)
	LIGHTWEIGHT			
(Newry)	Adrian Patterson	beat	Eamonn McEneaney	(Dundalk)
	LIGHT-WELTERWEIGHT			
(Cork)	Seán Barrett	beat	Paul McCloskey	(Dungiven)
	WELTERWEIGHT			
(St Paul's, Waterford)	Neil Gough	beat	James Moore	(Arklow)

	LIGHT-MIDDLEWEIGHT			
(Sunnyside, Cork)	Michael Roche	*beat*	John Duddy	(Derry)

	MIDDLEWEIGHT			
(St Colman's, Cork)	Kevin Walsh	*beat*	Ian Timms	(CIE)

	LIGHT-HEAVYWEIGHT			
(Sligo)	Alan Reynolds	*beat*	Seán O'Grady	(St Saviour's, Dublin)

	HEAVYWEIGHT			
(Sligo)	Stephen Reynolds	*beat*	Seán Power	(Tramore)

	SUPER-HEAVYWEIGHT		
(Crumlin)	John Kinsella	*walkover*	

ROCHE IRELAND'S ONLY QUALIFIER – SYDNEY OLYMPIC GAMES 2000

With the break-up of the old Soviet Union, the number of countries vying to send boxers to the Olympic Games increased significantly. Boxing was no exception and the Amateur International Boxing Association (AIBA) introduced qualifying tournaments in an attempt to limit the number of competitors at the Sydney Olympic Games. The net result was that light-middleweight Michael Roche of the Sunnyside Club in Cork was Ireland's only qualifier and his Olympics ended in his opening bout when he lost to Turkey's Fırat Karagöllü 17-4. Bernard Dunne had secured the first-reserve spot for the featherweight division and travelled with the Irish team to Sydney. He travelled in hope rather than expectation but there was to be no appearance for Dunne as all of the boxers in the division weighed in on time, fit and healthy.

REYNOLDS BROTHERS TO THE FORE – NATIONAL SENIOR FINALS 2001

It was an explosive family double for Sligo brothers Alan and Stephen Reynolds, who again claimed national titles at light-heavyweight and heavyweight respectively. Stephen was assured as he claimed his fifth successive title by stopping Dubliner Gary Dargan in the third round, while Alan secured a hat-trick of titles in spectacular fashion by flooring James Kelly with a peach of a left hook. One of the night's most impressive victors was Dundalk's Michael Kelly, the World Military Champion, who claimed his first senior title with an 11-4 win over Derry southpaw Paul McCloskey in an absorbing light-welterweight final. Teenager Kenny Egan was in superb form when he overcame Belfast's Conal Carmichael to clinch a first senior title for the Neilstown club in its twenty-one years of existence. Southpaw Egan displayed an excellent counter-punching style as he claimed his place in history alongside Ray Close, Wayne McCullough and Bernard Dunne by holding the national junior, intermediate and senior titles at the same time. Boxer of the Tournament went to James Moore, who showed skill and class as he dethroned Neil Gough in the welterweight final. The finals were attended by Hollywood movie star Matthew McConaughey, Taoiseach Bertie Ahern and boxing legend Barry McGuigan, who were thrilled by an excellent programme during which 1964 Olympian Seán McCafferty was inducted into the IABA Hall of Fame.

	LIGHT-FLYWEIGHT			
(Bray)	John Paul Kinsella	*beat*	Paul Baker	(Pegasus, Down)
	FLYWEIGHT			
(Saints, Belfast)	Liam Cunningham	*beat*	Darren Campbell	(Glin)
	BANTAMWEIGHT			
(Drogheda)	Damien McKenna	*beat*	Harry Cunningham	(Saints, Belfast)
	FEATHERWEIGHT			
(St Patrick's, Meath)	John Paul Campbell	*beat*	Kevin O'Hara	(Immaculata)
	LIGHTWEIGHT			
(Dockers)	Noel Monteith	*beat*	Eugene McEneaney	(Dundalk)
	LIGHT-WELTERWEIGHT			
(Dundalk)	Michael Kelly	*beat*	Paul McCloskey	(Dungiven)
	WELTERWEIGHT			
(Arklow)	James Moore	*beat*	Neil Gough	(St Paul's, Waterford)
	LIGHT-MIDDLEWEIGHT			
(Sunnyside, Cork)	Michael Roche	*beat*	John Duddy	(Ring, Derry)
	MIDDLEWEIGHT			
(Neilstown)	Kenny Egan	*beat*	Conal Carmichael	(Holy Trinity)
	LIGHT-HEAVYWEIGHT			
(St Joseph's, Sligo)	Alan Reynolds	*beat*	James Kelly	(Manorhamilton)
	HEAVYWEIGHT			
(St Joseph's, Sligo)	Stephen Reynolds	*beat*	Gary Dargan	(CIE)
	SUPER-HEAVYWEIGHT			
(Crumlin)	John Kinsella	*beat*	John Kiely	(Corpus Christi, Limerick)

LINDBURGH SHINES TO TAKE TITLE – NATIONAL SENIOR FINALS 2002

Arklow's James Moore, a bronze medallist at the 2001 World Championships, retained his welterweight title in the finals against David Conlon. The Dubliner put up a brave battle but was not powerful enough to prevent the industrious Arklow man from picking up the title with a third-round stoppage. The best performance of the night belonged to Drogheda's

Damien McKenna from the Holy Family club, who fought superbly in his bantamweight clash with Martin Lindsay. However, McKenna's exertions were surpassed by the stylish Lindsay, who took every opportunity to catch the Louth man. In a ding-dong of an all-Dublin light-flyweight final, Ballybrack's John Paul Kinsella got the better of Golden Cobra's Paul Hyland, winning on a deserved 10-7 scoreline. In a repeat of the 2001 flyweight final, Belfast's Liam Cunningham decisively outscored Dubliner Darren Campbell in a clash that was dictated by Cunningham's ability to open up Campbell's tight defence.

	LIGHT-FLYWEIGHT			
(Ballybrack)	John Paul Kinsella	*beat*	Paul Hyland	(Golden Cobra, Dublin)
	FLYWEIGHT			
(Saints)	Liam Cunningham	*beat*	Darren Campbell	(St Saviour's)
	BANTAMWEIGHT			
(Immaculata)	Martin Lindsay	*beat*	Damien McKenna	(Drogheda)
	FEATHERWEIGHT			
(Quarryvale, Dublin)	Stephen Ormond	*beat*	Gavin Brown	(Crumlin)
	LIGHTWEIGHT			
(Cavan/Clonoe)	Andrew Murray	*beat*	Noel Monteith	(Dockers, Belfast)
	LIGHT-WELTERWEIGHT			
(Dungiven)	Paul McCloskey	*beat*	Roy Sheehan	(St Michael's, Athy)
	WELTERWEIGHT			
(Arklow)	James Moore	*beat*	David Conlon	(Crumlin, Dublin)
	LIGHT-MIDDLEWEIGHT			
(Ring, Derry)	John Duddy	*beat*	Andrew Gibson	(Larne)
	MIDDLEWEIGHT			
(Neilstown)	Kenny Egan	*beat*	Marvin Lee	(Oughterard)
	LIGHT-HEAVYWEIGHT			
(Quarryvale, Dublin)	Ian Timms	*beat*	Michael McDonagh	(Brosna, Offaly)
	HEAVYWEIGHT			
(St Joseph's, Sligo)	Alan Reynolds	*beat*	Patrick Sharkey	(Crumlin)
	SUPER-HEAVYWEIGHT			
(St Colman's, Cork)	Eanna Falvey	*beat*	Cathal McMonagle	(Holy Trinity)

ANDY LEE BEATS EAMON O'KANE – NATIONAL SENIOR FINALS 2003

Limerick southpaw Andy Lee, a silver medallist in the World Junior Championships in Cuba in 2002 and reigning Irish 'Boxer of the Year', recorded an excellent 22-12 victory over Derry's Eamon O'Kane in the final of the middleweight class. London-born Lee was always in front with superb combinations that unravelled O'Kane's aggressive style. There was consolation for O'Kane's club, St Canice's, Dungiven, when Paul McCloskey showed the greater ambition to see off Dundalk's Michael Kelly in the light-welterweight decider. Belfast's Immaculata club had mixed fortunes also as Paul Baker took the honours in the light-flyweight division, but Martin Rogan was unlucky as he succumbed to Offaly's Thomas Crampton in the battle of the super-heavyweights.

	LIGHT-FLYWEIGHT			
(Immaculata)	Paul Baker	*beat*	John Paul Kinsella	(Ballybrack)
	FLYWEIGHT			
(Golden Cobra, Dublin)	Paul Hyland	*beat*	Thomas Lee	(Oughterard)
	BANTAMWEIGHT			
(Holy Trinity)	Brian Gillen	*beat*	Martin Lindsay	(Immaculata)
	FEATHERWEIGHT			
(Quarryvale, Dublin)	Stephen Ormond	*beat*	Eamonn Touhey	(Moate)
	LIGHTWEIGHT			
(Cavan)	Andrew Murray	*beat*	Garrett Dunne	(Neilstown, Dublin)
	LIGHT-WELTERWEIGHT			
(Dungiven)	Paul McCloskey	*beat*	Michael Kelly	(Dundalk)
	WELTERWEIGHT			
(Arklow)	James Moore	*beat*	Thomas Blaney	(Westside, Dublin)
	MIDDLEWEIGHT			
(St Francis, Limerick)	Andy Lee	*beat*	Eamon O'Kane	(Dungiven)
	LIGHT-HEAVYWEIGHT			
(Neilstown)	Kenny Egan	*beat*	Conal Carmichael	(Holy Trinity)
	HEAVYWEIGHT			
(St Joseph's, Sligo)	Alan Reynolds	*beat*	Thomas Donnelly	(Tyrone)
	SUPER-HEAVYWEIGHT			
(Offaly)	Thomas Crampton	*beat*	Martin Rogan	(Immaculata)

COYLE DETHRONES MOORE – NATIONAL SENIOR FINALS 2004

With the Olympic Games taking place in Athens in 2004, that year's senior finals took place at the stadium in December 2003. In a superb welterweight final, James Moore, one of Ireland's top Olympic hopes, was beaten sensationally by the determined Henry Coyle from Mayo in a battle that had the crowd on the edges of their seats. The score was even at 6-6 after the first two rounds, but Coyle rallied in the third to lead 11-10 and put in a storming finish to record a 17-12 verdict. Conor

Ahern, winner of a gold medal at the multi-nations tournament in Cork, won the light-flyweight title with a victory over Wicklow's Ross Hickey. Belfast featherweight Martin Lindsay made up for his loss in 2003 with a decisive 17-8 decision over Eamon Tuohey of Moate, while Dublin's Paul Hyland's attacking style was key in his 17-4 decision over Tommy Lee in the flyweight bout. Kenny Egan took his second successive light-heavyweight crown with a low-scoring 8-2 victory against Marvin Lee, a Galway Garda, who was named after the legendary 'Marvellous' Marvin Hagler. Future legend Andy Lee took the middleweight title by beating Dublin's Patrick Murray.

	LIGHT-FLYWEIGHT			
(Baldoyle)	Conor Ahern	beat	Ross Hickey	(Wicklow)
	FLYWEIGHT			
(Golden Cobra, Dublin)	Paul Hyland	beat	Thomas Lee	(Oughterard)
	BANTAMWEIGHT			
(St Michael's, Athy)	Eric Donovan	beat	Brian Gillen	(Holy Trinity)
	FEATHERWEIGHT			
(Immaculata, Belfast)	Martin Lindsay	beat	Eamon Touhey	(Moate)
	LIGHTWEIGHT			
(Cavan)	Andrew Murray	beat	Noel Monteith	(Dockers, Belfast)
	LIGHT-WELTERWEIGHT			
(Dungiven)	Paul McCloskey	beat	Michael Kelly	(Dundalk)
	WELTERWEIGHT			
(Geesala, Mayo)	Henry Coyle	beat	James Moore	(Arklow)
	MIDDLEWEIGHT			
(St Francis, Limerick)	Andy Lee	beat	Patrick Murray	(St Matthew's, Dublin)
	LIGHT-HEAVYWEIGHT			
(Neilstown)	Kenny Egan	beat	Marvin Lee	(Oughterard)
	HEAVYWEIGHT			
(St Joseph's, Sligo)	Alan Reynolds	beat	Michael McDonagh	(Brosna, Offaly)
	SUPER-HEAVYWEIGHT			
(Immaculata)	Martin Rogan	beat	Jimmy Upton	(Crumlin)

LEE IRELAND'S ONLY OLYMPIAN – ATHENS OLYMPIC GAMES 2004

Andy Lee was Ireland's sole boxing representative at the Atlanta Olympic Games in 2004. He assured his place after his bronze medal success in the European Championships in Croatia in March that year. Ireland had entered twelve boxers into the qualifying tournaments, but Lee was the only competitor to qualify. This had been especially disappointing for Irish boxing, especially as a High Performance Unit had been established after the Sydney Olympics. Born in Bow, London, Lee's family returned to Ireland in 1998 and took up residence in Castleconnell, County Limerick. Lee had boxed with his brothers Ned and Tommy at the Repton boxing club in London and then joined the St Francis club in Limerick city. In Athens, Lee beat Mexican Alfredo Angulo in the first round of the middleweight division. In his second outing, he faced Hassan N'Dam N'Jikam of Cameroon and the bout was adjudged as a draw, only for Lee to be beaten on a computerised countback decision.

IAN TIMMS' GREAT DISPLAY – NATIONAL SENIOR FINALS 2005

Dubliner Ian Timms caused a sensation in the 2005 finals when he outfoxed and out-boxed Ballina's Alan Reynolds, who was going for his seventh consecutive title, in the heavyweight decider. Timms, at 26, used his left jab to great effect to bamboozle the experienced Reynolds and ran out a 13-9 winner. In the bantamweight decider, David Oliver added the senior title to his junior and intermediate championships with a 22-6 win over Antrim's Shaun McKim. At light-flyweight, Conor Ahern of Baldoyle retained his crown with a third-round win over Limerick's Jimmy Moore, who was forced to take two standing counts before referee Peter Clifford intervened after one and a half minutes of the third. The undoubted class of Belfast's Carl Frampton shone through as he beat Wexford flyweight Derek Thorpe on a 14-4 score in the flyweight clash.

LIGHT-FLYWEIGHT				
(Baldoyle)	Conor Ahern	beat	Jimmy Moore	(St Francis, Limerick)
FLYWEIGHT				
(Midland White City)	Carl Frampton	beat	Derek Thorpe	(St Aidan's, Wexford)
BANTAMWEIGHT				
(St Michael's, Athy)	David Oliver Joyce	beat	Shaun McKim	(Antrim)
FEATHERWEIGHT				
(St Michael's, Athy)	Eric Donovan	beat	Eamon Touhey	(Moate)
LIGHTWEIGHT				
(St Matthew's, Dublin)	Stephen Ormond	beat	Dean Murphy	(St Saviour's)
LIGHT-WELTERWEIGHT				
(St Michael's, Athy)	David Oliver Joyce	beat	Keith Boyle	(St Saviour's)

	WELTERWEIGHT			
(St Saviour's)	Karl Brabazon	*beat*	Oisin Kelly	(Portlaoise)

	MIDDLEWEIGHT			
(St Francis, Limerick)	Andy Lee	*beat*	Eamon O'Kane	(Dungiven)

	LIGHT-HEAVYWEIGHT			
(Neilstown)	Kenny Egan	*beat*	Darren O'Neill	(Paulstown, Kilkenny)

	HEAVYWEIGHT			
(St Matthew's, Dublin)	Ian Timms	*beat*	Alan Reynolds	(Ballina)

	SUPER-HEAVYWEIGHT			
(Holy Trinity)	Cathal McMonagle	*beat*	Scott Belshaw	(Lisburn)

HAMILL BRINGS TITLE TO BALLYMENA – NATIONAL SENIOR FINALS 2006

Cavan's David Nevin was left disappointed after the 18-year-old southpaw went down to a 10-6 points defeat to the experienced Dermot Hamill from the All Saints club from Ballymena. The Cavan teenager had impressed on his way to the light-welterweight final, but came up against an opponent who frustrated the aggressive Nevin. Portlaoise duo Edward Healy and T.J. Doheny won many admirers at the National Stadium but both tasted defeat. Healy's bout with Darren Sutherland was stopped on the twenty-point rule, while Doheny was weakened by a bout of influenza in the week leading up to his contest with Baldoyle's Conor Ahern, but acquitted himself with style. Limerick's Jimmy Moore saw off Paddy Barnes by 12-10 in Barnes' first appearance in the senior finals. The Belfast boxer was to reverse that decision in the following year's final.

	LIGHT-FLYWEIGHT			
(St Francis, Limerick)	Jimmy Moore	*beat*	Paddy Barnes	(Holy Family)

	FLYWEIGHT			
(Baldoyle, Dublin)	Conor Ahern	*beat*	T.J. Doheny	(Portlaoise)

	BANTAMWEIGHT			
(St Michael's, Athy)	David Oliver Joyce	*beat*	Kevin Fennessy	(Clonmel)

	FEATHERWEIGHT			
(St Michael's, Athy)	Eric Donovan	*beat*	Ross Hickey	(Wicklow)

	LIGHTWEIGHT			
(St Michael's, Athy)	John Joe Joyce	*beat*	John Paul Campbell	(Edenderry)

	LIGHT-WELTERWEIGHT			
(All Saints, Ballymena)	Dermot Hamill	*beat*	David Nevin	(Cavan)

	WELTERWEIGHT			
(St Michael's, Athy)	Roy Sheahan	*beat*	David Oliver Joyce	(St Michael's, Athy)

MIDDLEWEIGHT				
(St Saviour's, Dublin)	Darren Sutherland	*beat*	Edward Healy	(Portlaoise)
LIGHT-HEAVYWEIGHT				
(Neilstown)	Kenny Egan	*beat*	Darren O'Neill	(Paulstown, Kilkenny)
HEAVYWEIGHT				
(St Joseph's, Sligo)	Alan Reynolds	*beat*	Ian Timms	(St Matthews, Dublin)
SUPER-HEAVYWEIGHT				
(Offaly)	Anthony Crampton	*beat*	Martin Sweeney	(Crumlin)

SUTHERLAND IMPRESSES – NATIONAL SENIOR FINALS 2007

Before a capacity crowd and live on RTÉ television, the 'Blanchardstown Bomber' Darren Sutherland retained his middleweight title by pounding out a victory over Dungiven's five-time Ulster champion Eamon O'Kane over three rounds at the National Stadium. Ireland's top amateur Kenny Egan was too skilful and experienced for Omagh's Willie Mitchell of the Shamrocks ABC and took his fifth national crown at light-heavy when he stopped Mitchell after twenty-two seconds of the first round. Belfast-based Letterkenny man Cathal McMonagle pulled out all the stops in the fourth round to clinch a victory over Anthony Crampton in a pulsating contest for the super-heavyweight title. However, there was disappointment for fellow Donegal boxer John Sweeney, who lost on points to St Matthew's heavyweight Ian Timms in a top-class bout which Timms took despite conceding points after receiving a public warning.

LIGHT-FLYWEIGHT				
(Holy Family)	Paddy Barnes	*beat*	Jimmy Moore	(St Francis, Limerick)
FLYWEIGHT				
(Baldoyle, Dublin)	Conor Ahern	*beat*	Shane Cox	(Gorey)
BANTAMWEIGHT				
(Immaculata, Belfast)	Ryan Lindberg	*beat*	Kevin Fennessy	(Clonmel)
FEATHERWEIGHT				
(St Michael's, Athy)	David Oliver Joyce	*beat*	Eric Donovan	(St Michael's, Athy)
LIGHTWEIGHT				
(St Michael's, Athy)	John Joe Joyce	*beat*	Ciaran Bates	(St Mary's, Dublin)
LIGHT-WELTERWEIGHT				
(Golden Cobra, Dublin)	Aodh Carlyle	*beat*	Thomas Dwyer	(Wexford)

	WELTERWEIGHT			
(St Michael's, Athy)	Roy Sheahan	*beat*	David Oliver Joyce	(St Michael's, Athy)

	MIDDLEWEIGHT			
(St Saviour's, Dublin)	Darren Sutherland	*beat*	Eamon O'Kane	(Immaculata)

	LIGHT-HEAVYWEIGHT			
(Neilstown)	Kenny Egan	*beat*	Willie Mitchell	(Tyrone)

	HEAVYWEIGHT			
(St Matthew's, Dublin)	Ian Timms	*beat*	John Sweeney	(Dungloe)

	SUPER-HEAVYWEIGHT			
(Holy Trinity)	Cathal McMonagle	*beat*	Anthony Crampton	(Offaly)

SUTHERLAND GRACIOUS IN VICTORY – NATIONAL SENIOR FINALS 2008

The most anticipated contest of the night pitted Darren Sutherland and Darren O'Neill against each other for the middleweight title. It was a tremendous bout, during which Sutherland came from 9-6 behind at the end of the second round to take the decision in the last two rounds. It was O'Neill's third senior final defeat, but Sutherland was gracious in victory, telling the crowd, 'At the end of the day, Ireland should be blessed: you have two world-class middleweights. We are both top ten in the world. Out of a small island like this and we are out there competing with the best in the world. You should be grateful.'

The heavyweight final at the 2008 senior finals brought together two fighters with almost matching surnames, Con Sheehan from Clonmel and Tommy Sheahan from Athy. It was an exhausting battle, which was won by 18-year-old Con, who booked his place on in the Olympic qualifiers in Italy at the end of February. At light-flyweight, Paddy Barnes, then Ireland's only representative at the Seoul Olympics, proved too crafty for Limerick's Jimmy Moore, who retired during the fourth round of the contest, having registered no points on the computerised system.

	LIGHT-FLYWEIGHT			
(Holy Family)	Paddy Barnes	*beat*	James Moore	(St Francis, Limerick)

	FLYWEIGHT			
(Gorey)	Shane Cox	*beat*	Ruairi Dalton	(Antrim)

	BANTAMWEIGHT			
(Cavan)	John Joe Nevin	*beat*	TJ Doheny	(Portlaoise)

	FEATHERWEIGHT			
(Athy)	David Oliver Joyce	*beat*	Kevin Fennessy	(Clonmel)

	LIGHTWEIGHT			
(Grangecon, Wicklow)	Ross Hickey	*beat*	Anthony Cacace	(Holy Trinity)

	LIGHT-WELTERWEIGHT			
(St Michael's, Athy)	John Joe Joyce	*beat*	Jamie Kavanagh	(Crumlin)

	WELTERWEIGHT			
(Athy)	Roy Sheehan	*beat*	John Joe McDonagh	(Brosna, Offaly)

	MIDDLEWEIGHT			
(St Saviour's)	Darren Sutherland	*beat*	Darren O'Neill	(Paulstown, Kilkenny)

	LIGHT-HEAVYWEIGHT			
(Neilstown)	Kenny Egan	*beat*	Ciaran Curtis	(Dundalk)

	HEAVYWEIGHT			
(Clonmel)	Con Sheehan	*beat*	Tommy Sheahan	(St Michael's, Athy)

	SUPER-HEAVYWEIGHT	
(Holy Trinity)	Cathal McMonagle	*walkover*

THE BEST SINCE MELBOURNE – BEIJING OLYMPIC GAMES 2008

Ireland took a team of five boxers of the 2008 Olympics and claimed three medals in what was a spectacular achievement. Paddy Barnes was the first Irish boxer to claim a place on the Irish team. He battled his way through a qualifying tournament in Chicago in October 2007 to take the light-flyweight position. In the finals he was afforded a bye in the opening round and made light work of Ecuador's José Meza to battle his way into the quarterfinal where a bronze medal was at stake. Standing in his way was the Pole Łukasz Maszczyk. However, Barnes made all the running during the bout and eased home on an 11-5 scoreline to take bronze. For Barnes though, the hometown favourite, China's Zou Shiming, stood in his way. In the end, Barnes was outboxed, but felt offended when the judges failed to award him a single point. His annoyance at this oversight was entirely justified, but, with hindsight, it was no disgrace. Zou was one of the classiest boxers of the tournament and took the gold medal with ease.

For Darren Sutherland, the 25-year-old from St Saviour's club, a bye in the opening round of the middleweight division saw him matched against Algeria's Nabil Kassel. The three-time Irish champion showed no mercy when he stopped his opponent in the fourth round to set up a bronze-medal bout with Venezuela's Alfonso Blanco. The fight was Sutherland's from start to finish, with the Dubliner recording an emphatic 11-1 victory to set up a fight with his old rival, James De Gale from Great Britain. The omens looked good for Sutherland. He had boxed the Englishman on five previous occasions, with the Dubliner winning four of those bouts. However, that pre-fight confidence was not to work in Sutherland's favour as he came up short against his old foe in the semi-final in a somewhat subdued performance. Soon Frank Maloney signed up the talented middleweight for what promised to be an exciting paid career in the professional ranks.

Kenny Egan's Olympics saw him fight on five occasions, only to lose to China's Xiaping Zhang in the light-heavyweight final. Julius Jackson of the Virgin Islands, Bahram Muzaffer of Turkey, Brazil's Washington Silva and Tony Jeffries of Great Britain were all defeated as Egan stormed his way to the final. Controversy though was the order of the day in the final. At the end of the third round, there was evidence that the judges failed to credit Egan with several scoring punches that would have put him ahead in the bout. This was a serious oversight and most neutral observers felt that the Irishman was denied the gold medal through the errors. Back in Ireland, bookmakers Paddy Power were not so restrained in their judging of the bout and paid out all bets on Egan. Following the final, President Mary McAleese and Taoiseach Brian Cowen paid tribute to the Irish captain for his bravery throughout the Olympics. The president said she was 'delighted to learn of Kenny's wonderful accomplishment today in Beijing. The people of Ireland are uplifted by this outstanding achievement, which continues a tradition of Irish Olympic boxing excellence dating back to 1952.'

JOHN JOE NEVIN SHOWS HIS CLASS – NATIONAL SENIOR FINALS 2009

With Darren Sutherland having turned professional, only four of Ireland's 2008 Olympians appeared in the national senior finals in 2009. For Paddy Barnes, though, it was merely to collect his light-flyweight crown, which he retained as that year's only entrant. Kenny Egan took a record equalling ninth title with a 10-6 victory over Belfast's Tommy McCarthy, while John Joe Joyce was knocked out by another protégé of the Sutcliffe clan, Philip. The performance of the night and the fans' Boxer of the Tournament belonged to Mullingar's John Joe Nevin, who overwhelmed former champion Ryan Lindberg of the Immaculata club on a 15-1 score line. At featherweight, Carl Frampton again made his mark on the national stage with an assured win over David Oliver Joyce to secure his second title.

	LIGHT-FLYWEIGHT			
(Holy Family)	Paddy Barnes *walkover*			

	FLYWEIGHT			
(Dublin Docklands)	Declan Geraghty	*beat*	Conor Ahern	(Baldoyle)

		BANTAMWEIGHT		
(Cavan)	John Joe Nevin	*beat*	Ryan Lindberg	(Immaculata)
		FEATHERWEIGHT		
(Midland White City)	Carl Frampton	*beat*	David Oliver Joyce	(Athy)
		LIGHTWEIGHT		
(Athy)	Eric Donovan	*beat*	Ross Hickey	(Wicklow)
		LIGHT-WELTERWEIGHT		
(Crumlin)	Philip Sutcliffe	*beat*	John Joe Joyce	(Athy)
		WELTERWEIGHT		
(Buncrana)	Willie McLoughlin	*beat*	Cathal McAuley	(Dungloe)
		MIDDLEWEIGHT		
(Kilkenny)	Darren O'Neill	*beat*	Stephen O'Reilly	(Ballybofey)
		LIGHT-HEAVYWEIGHT		
(Neilstown)	Kenny Egan	*beat*	Tommy McCarthy	(Oliver Plunkett)
		HEAVYWEIGHT		
(Clonmel)	Con Sheehan	*beat*	Alan Reynolds	(Sligo)
		SUPER-HEAVYWEIGHT		
(Moate)	David Joyce	*walkover*		

BERNARD DUNNE *v.* RICHARD CORDOBA

The magnificence of what occurred on Saturday 21 March 2009 in Dublin's O2 Arena was quite simply a thing of beauty; a joy forever. When sport can create moments of simple patriotic pleasure and mix it with pure theatre, it is a delight to behold. For Ireland, that day provided not one, but two memorable highs. In the late afternoon, the last-gasp drama of the country's grand slam rugby triumph in Cardiff set up Dunne's crack at glory later that evening perfectly. The euphoria of Ireland's victory created a feel-good factor across the island and the watching masses were not to be denied a further episode of greatness. For those fans of the noble art who wrote off Bernard Dunne's chances after he was defeated by Kiko Martinez, the third Saturday in March would prove to be redemption day for the Dublin Dynamo.

The Dubs were in fine voice as the 'Olé, Olé' began early. The mood was exuberant as the Irish rugby victory set the tone of the evening. The anticipation rose as the undercard progressed. In the main supporting bout, Andy Lee was to endure a tough ten-round encounter against Alex Sibos, but came through in the end on a 99-91 verdict. Despite the result, the Limerick man suffered a cut above his right eye during the first round that was a cause for concern in his corner. In the sixth, he dropped the German, who gamely fought on but, by taking all but one of the rounds, Lee was a comfortable winner whose performance was warmly received. The eye-opening performance of the night came in the form of the exhibition bout between world champions Katie Taylor and the American champion Caroline Barry. The crowd were truly impressed with the style and standard of the female version of the sport. Taylor hit the front in the opening round and controlled the bout for the full four rounds to win convincingly. In the commentary box, Dave 'Boy' McAuley, who had been sceptical previously of women's boxing, was duly won over by Taylor's display. Irish wins came also from the Cavan boxer Andy Murray, who took the European Union lightweight title, by beating defeating Daniel Rasilla on points. Meanwhile Paddy Barnes easily won his own exhibition bout while crowd favourite Jim Rock and Michael Kelly both won to make it a great night for the Irish. Dunne's moment arrived.

The dry ice, the Irish Rover, the anthem and the moment was emotional. It all came and went in a blur. After the drama of the build-up, the moment of truth arrived as the bell sounded. The fight began in a crescendo of noise with the taller Cordoba using his long jab to great effect to keep Dunne at bay. Soon the Dubliner began to make his mark with a couple of neat left hooks and combinations that shook Cordoba as he shortly lost his composure. By the third round, Cordoba recovered and took the fight to the challenger, boxing with renewed aggression. Soon, Dunne reacted and in the last half minute of the round came at Cordoba with vigour, planting a neat left hook to the champion's chin that had Cordoba on the canvas and the crowd on their feet. The referee began the count as Dunne sensed that Cordoba was there for the taking, but with only twelve seconds until the bell, Dunne had no time to capitalise on his advantage. The fight had reached the fourth round and Dunne, despite what the critics thought, was holding his own with the champion. The expectation in the arena was growing. In the corner between rounds, Harry Hawkins exuded extreme calmness as he tended to Dunne; it was a fight that was there for the taking. In the fourth, the complexion of the fight changed by a clash of heads which left Dunne with a cut. Regardless, Dunne threw some excellent left hooks, but the champion began to show some neat touches as he regained the upper hand. The crowd began to rally behind Dunne as it became evident that the Dubliner was going to have to fight tooth and nail to see off the craft and skill of Cordoba.

However, for all the good work of Dunne, the fifth round was almost disastrous for him. The round began with a Cordoba slip and, despite the roars of the crowd, the champion began to gain the upper hand. As 9,037 spectators watched helplessly, Cordoba opened up and, just a minute into the round, Dunne was knocked to the canvas for the first time. The signs were ominous as the undoubted boxing skill of the champion came to the fore and Dunne began to look somewhat dishevelled. After the count, Dunne tried to mix it with the champion but soon found himself on the end of another fast combination that sent him to the canvas for the second time. The battered and bloodied Dubliner was almost finished. The crowd roared encouragement and the round ended with Dunne hanging on for dear life on the ropes as Cordoba went for broke. The champion fired at least sixteen clean shots that landed on Dunne. It was a vicious onslaught. At this stage, nobody would have argued with the referee if he had have called a halt to proceedings. He hesitated and Dunne was literally saved by the bell. It had been a massive round for the champion and it seemed the clock was ticking for Bernard's title hopes. There was work to do in the Dunne's corner as it seemed that the fight was slipping away from the challenger.

For Dunne, composure was now the name of the game as the bell sounded for the sixth round. Keeping the champion at a distance was vital and Dunne threw his own combinations as his confidence returned. He survived the sixth and in the seventh he began to reassert himself in the contest. It seemed that Cordoba's best shots had been absorbed by Dunne and the fight was still in the melting pot. As the eighth began, Dunne looked refreshed and matched the champion blow for blow. The champion knew that, if the fight went the distance, he could be in trouble as Dunne seemed to be growing in confidence and showing extraordinary fitness and durability. The champion came forward to try to take the fight to the Dubliner, but Dunne was fighting the bout of his life in front of a crowd whose expectations were growing by the minute. In the tenth round, Cordoba was dominant and forced Dunne to display his skill at counter-punching. Cordoba again launched a flurry of body shots as the round ended with Dunne pinned to the ropes. Yet the Irishman refused to yield to the onslaught as the fans roared encouragement. The bell sounded. Dunne was going nowhere and Cordoba knew it. Far away from his native Panama, he was alone in an arena of noise. Dunne was not going to give up easily as he had waited all his life for the chance to fight for a world title. The tide was turning and the end was close at hand.

By the eleventh round, both men were practically out on their feet. The fight had now entered the category of a boxing classic and, as every minute passed, it was improving in its greatness. Punches, uppercuts, jabs and hooks continued to be thrown at a tremendous pace as the fight went one way and then the other. With a minute left in the round, Dunne produced the punch that sent the champion to the floor for the second time. The crowd was ecstatic, but the champion was back on his feet quickly and, after the count, the order to 'box on' was given. Dunne was straight in and soon Cordoba was on the canvas again as the clock showed forty-five seconds to go in the round. Dunne was just seconds away from glory. Cordoba was out on his feet. The referee thought about stopping the fight, but then thought again – the end was near. Accuracy, power, skill, belief and stamina had got Dunne to the threshold of the world title and he could almost taste the glory. Cordoba was a beaten man. The crowd sensed it, his corner sensed it, but Bernard Dunne knew it. As Cordoba heard the words 'box on', it was to be for the final time. He hit the canvas within seconds and that was that. It was over. The greatest moment of Bernard Dunne's sporting life had arrived.

In Irish sport, there have been far too few moments of pure euphoria. However, to have two such memorable events within the space of four hours was just phenomenal. The Irish rugby team had started the ball rolling and Dunne had completed an almost unbelievable day. Amid the chaotic scenes in the ring, Dunne was mobbed as he received the belt, announcing that his victory was dedicated to the whole of Ireland.

Showing emotion and humanity, he checked on the condition of Ricardo Cordoba, who had remained prone in the ring after being knocked out. Indeed, there were concerns for the Panamanian's well-being as medics worked frantically to revive him. Eventually there was movement from Cordoba and he was removed from the ring by stretcher and taken to hospital. It was reported soon after that he had made a full recovery but the manner in which he left the arena impacted somewhat on the Dunne victory. The referee was, however, coming in for some well-deserved criticism for the manner in which he had let the champion continue when it had been obvious that he was finished after the first knockdown of the last round. Dunne was enjoying his time in the packed ring as he received the belt and basked in the glory of the crowd. Almost sixty-one years to the day from when Rinty Monaghan claimed the world crown in Belfast's King's Hall, Ireland had a new champion. Dunne had scaled the heights, defeated his demons and proved he was the best. The fans eventually left the arena and the partying continued well into the small hours.

The reality for Bernard Dunne was that the only way he was going to win the contest as it entered the eleventh round was by a knockout. Whatever was said in the corner at the end of the tenth round obviously worked its magic. It was a truly epic end to a fight in which Dunne trailed. As *Fightnews.com* was to report, 'Dunne's Irish heart was just unstoppable on this night. He fought back and the war continued, both men giving no quarter. At the start of the eleventh round, Cordoba was ahead on the scorecards 95-92, 96-91, 97-90 and the title seemed headed back to Panama. However, the champion was exhausted and Dunne came out like a predator, sensing that he needed a knockout. Dunne battered Cordoba, floored him three times and made Ireland proud. An incredible turnabout.' Within the Brian Peters camp, it was total satisfaction. He had taken the gamble of the title fight and worked his magic to pull off one of the greatest shows in Irish sporting history. Bernard Dunne had paid Peters back in kind for his faith in him. After taking the criticism on the chin for far too long, Peters relished the post-fight press conference afterwards and, with great pride, he told the assembled hacks, 'Tonight was the biggest financial gamble of my life. There were a lot of naysayers out there. All I can say is, "O ye of little faith".'

RECORD EQUALLED BY MAGICAL KEN – NATIONAL SENIOR FINALS 2010

Kenny Egan was crowned Irish senior champion for a record-breaking tenth successive time, following a hard-fought win over Belfast light-heavyweight Tommy McCarthy. The Neilstown southpaw claimed an 8-5 decision in a repeat of the 2009 final, which the Olympic silver medallist had won 9-5. Egan's achievement equalled Mick Dowling's record of eight consecutive titles at the same weight, which had been set between 1968 and 1975, and emulated Jim O'Sullivan's run of ten titles between 1980 and 1990. O'Sullivan presented Egan with his belt and trophy inside the ring. Beijing Olympian John Joe Joyce defeated defending champion Willie McLaughlin to claim the welterweight title after a tight contest which was level at 6-6 at the end of the second. The bill was graced also by world and European champion Katie Taylor, who won claimed a 10-2 victory in a bout with 2009 European finalist Julia Tsyplakova from the Ukraine.

	LIGHT-FLYWEIGHT			
(Holy Family)	Paddy Barnes	*beat*	James Moore	(St Francis, Limerick)
	FLYWEIGHT			
(Moate)	Gary Molloy	*beat*	Conor Ahern	(Baldoyle, Dublin)
	BANTAMWEIGHT			
(Cavan)	John Joe Nevin	*beat*	Derek Thorpe	(St Aidan's, Wexford)
	FEATHERWEIGHT			
(Buncrana)	Tyrone McCullough	*beat*	James Fryers	(Immaculata)
	LIGHTWEIGHT			
(Athy)	Eric Donovan	*beat*	David Oliver Joyce	(Athy)
	LIGHT-WELTERWEIGHT			
(Westport)	Ray Moylette	*beat*	Stephen Donnelly	(All Saints, Ballymena)
	WELTERWEIGHT			
(St Michael's, Athy)	John Joe Joyce	*beat*	Willie McLaughlin	(Buncrana)

	MIDDLEWEIGHT			
(Paulstown)	Darren O'Neill	*beat*	Jason Quigley	(Ballybofey)

	LIGHT-HEAVYWEIGHT			
(Neilstown)	Kenny Egan	*beat*	Tommy McCarthy	(Oliver Plunkett)

	HEAVYWEIGHT			
(Clonmel)	Con Sheehan	*beat*	Alan Reynolds	(St Joseph's, Sligo)

	SUPER-HEAVYWEIGHT			
(Holy Trinity)	Cathal McMonagle	*beat*	Tommy Sheahan	(Athy)

EGAN HUMBLED BY RISING STAR –
NATIONAL SENIOR FINALS 2011

Ross Hickey was most impressive at the 2011 National Championships finals night after claiming the light-welterweight title and picking up the Boxer of the Tournament accolade. A neat display of hard punching by Hickey saw off Crumlin's Philip Sutcliffe (son of Philip senior) in a display that brought delight to Hickey's supporters. Heavyweight Con Sheehan impressed with a 9-3 victory over Patrick Corcoran, with the Clonmel man storming from behind to take his fourth consecutive title. Defending super-heavyweight champion Cathal McMonagle's performance was eye-catching as he defeated Athlone's Kenny Okungbowa, who was making his debut in a senior final. However, the performance of the night belonged to 17-year-old Joe Ward, the previous year's AIBA world youth champion, who battered his way to an 11-6 win over Ken Egan, who was aiming for his eleventh senior titles in a row. Egan went down twice because of left hooks from Ward and received a public warning for dropping his head and shoulders.

	LIGHT-FLYWEIGHT			
(Holy Family)	Paddy Barnes	*beat*	Evan Metcalfe	(Crumlin)

	FLYWEIGHT			
(St John Bosco)	Michael Conlan	*beat*	Chris Phelan	(Newbridge)

	BANTAMWEIGHT			
(Cavan)	John Joe Nevin	*beat*	Tyrone McCullagh	(Holy Family)

	LIGHTWEIGHT			
(St Mary's, Dublin)	Michael McDonagh	*beat*	David Oliver Joyce	(Athy)

	LIGHT-WELTERWEIGHT			
(Grangecon/Army)	Ross Hickey	*beat*	Philip Sutcliffe	(Crumlin)

	WELTERWEIGHT			
(Bray)	Adam Nolan	*beat*	Karl Brabazon	(St Saviour's)

	MIDDLEWEIGHT			
(Paulstown)	Darren O'Neill	*beat*	Jason Quigley	(Ballybofey)

	LIGHT-HEAVYWEIGHT			
(Moate)	Joe Ward	*beat*	Kenny Egan	(Neilstown)

	HEAVYWEIGHT			
(Clonmel)	Con Sheehan	*beat*	Patrick Corcoran	(Olympic)

	SUPER-HEAVYWEIGHT			
(Holy Trinity)	Cathal McMonagle	*beat*	Kenny Okungbowa	(Athlone)

MCCLOSKEY STOPPED BY CUT EYE IN MANCHESTER

Dungiven's Paul McCloskey's clash with the WBA light-welterweight champion Amir Khan on 16 April 2011 ended after six lacklustre rounds when the referee stopped the fight as blood poured from a cut above the Derry man's eyes. The accidental clash of heads, in front of 17,000 spectators at the Manchester Evening News Arena, prompted Luis Pabon to summon the ringside doctor, Phil Sahu, who ordered that the fight be stopped since McCloskey's vision was impaired by the blood. It was then left to the judges to deem that Khan was the unanimous winner.

As the underdog, McCloskey had been second best in the opening six rounds. However, a patient start to the fight was a key tactic for the McCloskey camp. McCloskey, the European champion, who had an unbeaten twenty-two-fight record, was incensed that the fight doctor had denied his corner men a chance to patch up the cut. Trainer John Breen, who was livid, told the media, 'Paul McCloskey hadn't started to work hard; the second half of the fight was the point when it was going to be his fight and he was denied the chance to win the world title by the doctor. The doctor beat Paul, not Khan.' McCloskey's manager, Barry Hearn, climbed into the ring shouting, 'You're a disgrace', while gesticulating towards the doctor. Paul McCloskey told reporters, 'I've been waiting for this fight my whole life and it has been taken away from me by a doctor. My corner men were not even given a chance to work on it. I am shocked and I am numb. It's ridiculous.'

Paul announced his retirement from boxing in September 2014. He had stopped Colin Lynes to claim the British super-lightweight title in December 2008, while a year later he beat Daniel Rasilla to take the European title in Magherafelt. On retiring, he expressed his regret at the disputed loss to Khan. 'You need luck at times and I maybe did not get that rub of the green when I needed it,' he said. 'I believe I had the talent and the ability to get my hands on a world title, but it was not meant to be.'

KATIE THRILLS A NATION
LONDON OLYMPIC GAMES 2012

The Irish boxing team at the 2012 London Olympic Games returned home with a haul of one gold, one silver and two bronze medals. The undoubted star of the team was Bray's Katie Taylor who captivated the nation and realised her dream by claiming gold in the 60kg class. That winning display on 9 August brought Ireland to a virtual standstill as Katie sealed her victory with a superb display to outpoint Russia's Sofya Ochigava on a 10-8 scoreline. As reigning world champion, Katie had fought her way to the final with an opening victory over Great Britain's Natasha Jonas and secured bronze by defeating Tajikistan's Mavzuna Chorieva. In the final, the 26-year-old was cheered on by thousands of excited Irish fans in London's ExCeL Arena and in towns across the country. Her win was truly memorable and was greeted by magnificent scenes, especially in her hometown of Bray. President Michael D. Higgins spoke for the nation when he said, 'She truly deserves this historic and hard earned victory; it is a just reward for her dedication and commitment over the years.'

In the men's competition, John Joe Nevin was denied a gold medal in the final of the bantamweight class when he lost out to Great Britain's Luke Campbell on a 14-11 scoreline. That fight was keenly contested and the Mullingar man found himself on the canvas in the last round, but fought back with gusto to lose gallantly after what had been a classic bout.

Following on from his success in Beijing, Paddy Barnes became the first Irish boxer to win medals at consecutive Olympics as he fought his way to bronze in the light-flyweight division. The Holy Family clubman had enjoyed victories over Thomas Essomba (15-10) and Devendro Singh Laishram (23-18) to set up a semi-final against China's Zou Shiming. Trailing going into the last round, Barnes fought courageously to draw level with his opponent at the final bell. However, he was to lose out by the narrowest of margins (45-44) on the computerised count back.

Belfast's Michael Conlan followed in the fine tradition of the St John Bosco club in Belfast to claim a bronze medal in the flyweight division. Conlon defeating Duke Micah (19-8) and Nordine Oubaali (22-18) to set up a semi-final against the Cuban Robeisy Ramirez Carrazana, but was to lose on a 20-10 margin. Wexford's Adam Nolan, a Garda officer and club mate of Katie Taylor in Bray, won his opening bout at welterweight against Equador's Carlos Sanchez Estacio (14-8) only to lose his next bout to bronze medallist Andrey Zamkovoy. Ireland's other competitor, Darren O'Neill, captained the side and enjoyed a victory in his opening fight against Muideen Akanji (15-6) before losing to Germany's Stefan Hartel by 19-12.